Contents

Acknowledgements

Staff and adopters who appear in the training film

David Akinsanya, adoption and fostering campaigner
and presenter for the series
Stephen Briers, Chartered Psychologist
Vivienne Henningham, Social Worker, Parents for
Children (now TACT)
Teresa Kennedy, Senior Social Work Practitioner,
St Francis' Children's Society
Rebecca May, Adoption Social Worker,
Northamptonshire Children and Young People's service
Cathy and Richard (and their daughter)
John and Anthony
Rachel (and her brother)
Suma and Albert (and their children)

We are also very grateful to the young people, children
and their parents, both in front of the camera and
behind it, who made such an important contribution to
the film.

Contributors to the workbook

Thanks are due to the following colleagues for their
guidance during the writing of this accompanying
workbook. They were all heavily involved in the original
TV series, *Find Me a Family*, and many of the imaginative
additional exercises and good ideas in this book come
from them:

Mo O'Reilly, Director of Child Placement at BAAF and
consultant to the TV series
Sue Lowe, Adoption Team Manager, Northamptonshire
Children and Young People's service
Christine Smith, Chief Executive Officer, St Francis'
Children's Society

Additional input which was also very helpful came from
Teresa Kennedy at St Francis and Rebecca May, Melanie
Sweeney and Karen Theobald, Northamptonshire.

Shaila Shah, BAAF's Director of Publications, has been,
as always, a great project manager to work with. Thank
you Shaila.

Jennifer Cousins, November 2009

The author

Jennifer Cousins is consultant to BAAF's
Opening Doors Disability Project, which aims to
help agencies develop new and more effective
ways to find permanent families for disabled
children. She has been a trainer and consultant
with BAAF since 1997.

Jennifer has extensive practice experience in
adoption and fostering, and children's disability.
For many years she chaired an adoption and
fostering panel. During 2007 and 2009 she
was part of a small international team working
in Romania to strengthen their domestic
adoption system, and then to develop foster
care training.

Jennifer has published a number of articles and
books, including the controversial article, 'Are
we missing the match? Rethinking adopter
assessment and child profiling' (*Adoption &
Fostering* 27:4, 2000). She is the author of
BAAF's Good Practice Guide on the placement
of disabled children, *Every Child is Special*
(2006), *Ten Top Tips for Finding Families for
Children* (2008), and 'Disability: still taboo in
family placement?' (*Adoption & Fostering* 33:2,
2009).

To find out more about the Opening Doors
Disability Project please go to
www.openingdoors.baaf.org.uk/

PUSHING THE BOUNDARIES OF ASSESSMENT

New techniques for preparing applicants and evidencing "suitability"

Jennifer Cousins

With contributions from

Sue Lowe, Adoption Team Manager, Northamptonshire County
Council **Mo O'Reilly**, Director of Child Placement, BAAF, **Christine
Smith**, Chief Executive Officer, St. Francis' Children's Society.

Published by
British Association for Adoption & Fostering (BAAF)
Saffron House
6–10 Kirby Street
London EC1N 8TS

www.baaf.org.uk

Charity registration 275689 (England and Wales) and SC039337 (Scotland)

British Library Cataloguing in Publication Data
A catalogue record for this book is available from the British Library

ISBN 978 1 905664 86 3

Editorial project management by Shaila Shah
Cover photographs posed by models, © iStockphoto.com
Designed by Helen Joubert Design
Printed in Great Britain by The Lavenham Press, Suffolk

BAAF is the leading UK-wide membership organisation for all those concerned
with adoption, fostering and child care issues.

Where all this started

Find Me a Family – the TV series

The Channel 4 TV series, *Find Me a Family*, in 2009 was inspired by the acknowledged mismatch between what adopters and foster carers want and the type of children who need new families – leaving many children unplaced and in limbo. The project was developed over a two-year period in collaboration with BAAF and the adoption teams of Northamptonshire Children and Young People's service, St Francis' Children's Society, and Parents for Children (now TACT).

The principal aims of the *Find Me a Family* series were:

a)   to broaden people's minds to the kind of children who need adoptive families – and essentially to tackle the mismatch;

b)   to show the public what the assessment process is about and to dispel some of the common myths.

The films had such an impact in the adoption world when they were broadcast in 2009 that it was felt that the training and assessment techniques developed during the project should be made more widely available to placement agencies across the UK: hence the short training film you are about to see, and which is available as a DVD, on the inside back cover.

The predominant issue addressed in this film is around the mismatch which disadvantages

disabled children and older, complex children. Black and minority ethnic children also wait a long time for a suitable family, a subject which is acknowledged in this workbook. Black and minority ethnic children of course can also bring the added complexities of age, difficult previous experiences and disability.

The techniques and the variants described here not only give prospective adopters and foster carers a real sense of the task ahead, but they also provide social workers with insights into the applicants' motivation, personality and lifestyle which, arguably, do not always emerge through current techniques. They are certainly thought-provoking and inspiring. Crucially, they provide assessors with evidence of applicants' suitability to take on this life-changing role – evidence that will form such an important part of the final reports for panel, and for a subsequent match.

Although the families seen in the films are all potential adopters, the techniques shown here, and most of the main messages, apply equally well to permanent foster carers. However, for the sake of brevity, the terms "adoption", "adopters" and sometimes "applicants" will mainly be used in Chapters 2–6 of this workbook.

Chapter 1
Introduction

The process of becoming an adopter or foster carer is one of the most testing personal journeys anyone can embark upon. It is challenging, both emotionally and intellectually, and demands honesty, resilience and the capacity for self-reflection and growth. People describe it as 'jumping through hoops'; as 'riding an emotional roller-coaster'; as 'learning things about themselves they hadn't really known before'. Hopefully, prospective adopters and foster carers emerge from the process not just older, but wiser and more open to the possibilities ahead. The incentive, of course, is the ultimate reward of becoming a family for the first time, or extending their existing family. From the agency's point of view, the goal is to create a new permanent family for a child in care.

In the past, that journey towards adoption consisted largely of discrete processes of preparation, assessment and matching, conducted by professionals. More recently, the greater involvement of the applicants has to some extent democratised this process: applicants are helped to understand how their own strengths and potential might be developed to match the needs of children in care and, eventually, one (two or three) specific children. This empowerment model is the underlying perspective of this project and accompanying training film.

A judgment about whether a person can do a job is surely only possible if the person understands what the job involves. So the more the assessment includes an exploration of the reality of children's lives, the more the applicant's history, lifestyle and personality can be set against this and discussed further. Hence it is crucial that the processes of learning about the "task" and assessment for suitability are combined.

The final element – matching – is the most problematic. Applicants can be assessed as suitable to adopt or foster and then wait months or years to be placed with a child. Many factors come into play: chance, agency policy, prejudice within the system, and applicants' lack of confidence and narrowness of vision. The first, no one can influence; the second (particularly where it centres on racial and cultural matching) is often the subject of protracted debate; the third (prejudice) is entrenched; the last (applicants' fear of uncertainty) can be tackled: minds can be broadened, solutions explored and confidence boosted. This is why good preparation and assessment are said to be developmental processes: adopters and foster carers who start with a cautious view about the kind of child they could take can, with input and support, have their eyes opened to their own abilities to take a very different kind of child – the children with particular difficulties, so many of whom wait in care for very long periods. How to accomplish this broadening and stretching of applicants' vision is the subject of this training film.

The mismatch

But first, a word or two about the notorious mismatch.

A snapshot of statistics for England shows that there are around 60,000 children in care, and that each year about 3,000 are adopted. This much is known from government statistics. What is not known is either the number of children awaiting adoption at any one point, or the number awaiting permanent fostering placements. Some estimates put this total at around 4,000.

The problem with reviewing research and quoting statistics in this field is that the unwary can discover they are comparing data about different groups of children in different parts of the UK: there is very little comparable information. One of the few sources of data about children and families waiting to be matched is the Adoption Register for England and Wales (Department for Education and Skills, 2007) – though even here, readers must understand that these are children and families who cannot be matched in-house or through local consortia (where again the data are not nationally co-ordinated). There are also helpful statistics from BAAF's family-finding newspaper and online service *Be My Parent* (www. bemyparent.org.uk/info-for-agencies/statistics/) – but again these are children for whom workers have not been able to find local families. The other useful data are from research on adoptions in England published by BAAF (Ivaldi, 2000); from a small local authority survey (Simon and Dance, 2006); from a study on the placement of black and minority ethnic children (Selwyn and Wijedasa, 2009); and from very limited government statistics. All these references are given in full later in this workbook. From these sources the issues that face family placement workers can only be described in broad, rather tentative terms.

The starting point for many who enquire about adoption is that they would ideally want a young child, and often would feel more confident about adopting a girl rather than a boy. Many of the children needing families, however, are aged 6–10, with more than half being boys. It is self-evident that the longer a child has been subjected to neglect, abuse and multiple moves, the more difficulties the child will bring into their new family – developmental, emotional and behavioural. So it is easy to see why prospective families who are new to these things want children whom they believe will bring less of this "baggage".

In terms of disability, which causes major concern for family-finders, only one in eight adoptive families say they could take a child with learning difficulties, and one in five a child with a physical impairment, though as many as 40 per cent of children waiting for families have some degree of impairment or "special need". It is thought that children under 2½ with developmental difficulties (especially boys) wait a long time, although there is some concern that the term "developmental delay" may not be sufficiently understood (*Be My Parent,* 2009). Children with severe medical problems wait twice as long as others – particularly boys and children over 2½.

People also prefer to take single children, whereas many children who need families come into care with siblings.

It is known that black and minority ethnic (BME) children are over-represented in the care system but are generally less likely than white children to be adopted, particularly the older age-range. A study by the Adoption Register found that, of the 36 minority ethnic children referred during one week in 2005, half were still waiting for a family a year later and therefore would be unlikely to be adopted (Selwyn and Wijedasa, 2009, p368). The Register's statistics also show that, while nearly a third of all referrals in 2006 were of minority ethnic children, only 17 per cent of adopters on the Register were from a BME background: another example of the infamous mismatch.

Children of *mixed* ethnicity, who form the majority of BME children in the care system, are not a homogenous group: they come from a very wide variety of ethnic backgrounds and although often entering care very young, pose real challenges to social workers at the matching stage. The profession remains in a quandary about how to place these children appropriately, which in itself causes delay and increased risk of failure to place. Agencies differ from each other in their policies and practice tendencies on the issue of so called "same-race" placements; and indeed, with the increasing complexity of children's racial, cultural and religious heritage, in deciding what kind of match would be best – or least problematic. Therefore for some adopters and permanent carers who respond to the profile of a child from a different racial or ethnic background to their own, their expression of interest would be immediately discouraged while others, applying to a neighbouring agency, may meet with a more nuanced reception. In the past five or so years there have been moves towards this more individualised and subtle approach, with consideration being given to the wider milieu in which the child would be brought up. The extended family, friendship network, local community, attitudes and experiences of a family who did not exactly match a child's ethnic mix would now be given more credence. But this remains a complex and contentious subject across the family placement world, with children often waiting for long periods for an unrealistically "perfect match". Where white foster carers apply to keep their BME foster child for adoption or permanence, the dilemma is often heightened by the fact of existing attachment.

The result of all these complexities is that even though the numbers of families and children on the Adoption Register's "actively waiting" lists are roughly similar (currently this equalizes at around 1,000 each) – the problem of the mismatch persists. The sad truth is that most families who are considering adoption or permanence do not envisage taking an older, complex child, and the real task therefore becomes how to support and encourage families to believe they could do it.

Everything which flows from this depends upon the quality of the social worker's assessment and the learning offered to applicants.

Assessment

Even though it is argued here that the processes of assessment, preparation and matching should in practice be integrated, it

may be helpful to explore each individually. Firstly then – assessment.

In summary, assessment is designed to:

- understand the strengths and weaknesses of the applicant/s and to form a view about their capacity to care for a child – their "suitability";

- assess the stability and permanence of the relationship, where a couple are applying;

- assess the robustness of the support network;

- identify areas where the applicant may benefit from further development, including the provision of post-placement support;

- enable the assessor to prepare the final report and make a proposal to panel about the applicant's suitability either to adopt or foster a child.

Assessment is a skilled job – it is not a case of writing down what applicants say and filling in forms. All the information about people's background, lifestyle, personality, attitudes, skills and relationships has to be sifted, evaluated and analysed. Ultimately a judgment is reached solely on whether the applicants can do the job of looking after someone else's child, not on whether they live traditional or unconventional lifestyles or hold minority opinions. This assessment task is complex, and therefore supervision that is both challenging and supportive is vital. Social workers preparing the key reports in adoption must be qualified to do so.

Most children requiring placement have experienced a variety of trauma: always through loss, often through abuse and neglect, sometimes through substance poisoning before birth; occasionally through the impact of hereditary conditions or disabilities. Adopters and foster carers must be sufficiently grounded and empathetic to stabilise and nurture these inevitably damaged children – with a combination of particular skills, personality attributes, knowledge, self-awareness and humility. For the assessor, all this must be taken into account and evidenced, and set against legislative requirements and standards.

As much as possible during the assessment should be transparent, and everything should be informative and run co-operatively. If people can't all work together, things will almost certainly fall apart. Nevertheless, however co-operative the relationship between applicants and social workers should ideally be, the final responsibility for the future safety and care of children lies with the professional staff. Their role in investigating applicants' safety as future parents or carers, through assessing their background and parenting capacity, confers a massive responsibility – a responsibility which cannot be dodged, or camouflaged by a friendly relationship.

It is inevitable and appropriate therefore that applicants have limited power in this daunting, highly-charged process on which the shape of their future life depends. Applicants feel under pressure to prove they are suitable, to say the right thing (whatever that might be) and to toe the line without complaint. Some feel doubly disadvantaged by being in a minority due, for example, to "race" or class or sexual orientation or disability status. This is uncomfortable – not the best position to be in when under scrutiny. Social workers are therefore charged with a delicate task: how to provide a supportive, informative relationship within which applicants can reflect on whether this is the right path for them, without feeling judged.

In the past this assessment process has often taken place through face-to-face discussions in the applicant's home – which is why it is called the home study. There is certainly value in being able to observe this setting. For example, to what extent do the applicants prefer order to disorder? How safety-conscious are they? To what degree is space shared or individualised? What do you notice about possessions, food, books, and animals? Who calls or rings when you are there? How do they (or the individual) deal with the unexpected? Over a number of visits, these observations may form a pattern which you can discuss. But on the applicants'

territory you are essentially their guest, and raising uncomfortable challenges is more difficult when social convention dictates that guests are ineffably polite.

An alternative is to invite applicants to an office. Here the power shifts even more towards the social worker, and under this pressure, different aspects of the applicants may be revealed. It is arguably easier for the social worker to resist collusion; and it would be more comfortable for a partner to discuss their "other half" in a neutral space. A combination of home and office may be ideal.

But with both these "talking" options, much rests on applicants' ability to reflect on and describe openly what they are like: their views, opinions, predispositions, strengths and weaknesses. More than this, they are being asked how, hypothetically, they would react in certain stressful situations in the future – as managing the inevitable stress will be a crucial factor in the success or failure of a placement. Faced with this question, and with so much at stake, surely applicants are tempted to paint the optimum picture? People rarely set out to lie, but self-perception may be distorted. In addition, people:

- tend to tell assessors what they want to hear;

- don't want to fail;

- may not understand what assessors want to know;

- are unsure what is relevant;

- may have a partner who does not know everything about them;

- may indeed have something to hide.

So, if assessment is essentially about getting to the bottom of understanding a person's personality and capacities, simply talking on the sofa will not be enough: somehow assessors need to "surprise the unconscious" – find out the individual default position to which everyone instinctively reverts under pressure. This will then provide some insight into how the applicants will react not only if the child pushes them to the limit, but also in everyday situations where parents have to think on their feet, problem-solve and co-operate with each other. Therefore a whole range of tools and exercises are needed, not just talking. Some of the thinking behind this is reflected in the competence model of assessment which requires externally validated evidence about applicants' abilities – not just through referees' opinions but through demonstration.

If, for example, assessors accompanied applicants around a supermarket on a Friday night before a bank holiday with a small child, they would soon know how the applicants really managed stress! – how patient they are; whether they have ideas about diversionary tactics to calm the frantic child; how they set boundaries (that endless aisle of sweets – oh dear); how they use reward mechanisms without bribes or empty threats – and so on. This would probably be quite different from the calm description in the peace of the living room during a home study visit.

Models of assessment

"Talking on the sofa" using the home study guidance in the BAAF Form F (Fostering) and the Prospective Adopter's Report ("PAR")[1] is not the only format for assessment. Models have developed over the years, which, with appropriate training, can be valuably used in combination. Models include:

- The traditional, individual psychodynamic perspective, which explores the impact of early experiences on current thinking and behaviour; it is less concerned with a social or cultural analysis.

- The ecological approach, which locates the individual in the context of their family, community and culture (for example, using *The Framework for the Assessment of Children in Need and their Families* which was developed to assess the here and now of caring for a child in the community; see Department of Health, 2000).

- Adult attachment interviews (AAI) and attachment-style interviews (ASI). These produce an evidenced profile of the applicant's fundamental pattern of responding to relationships that will be triggered when that adult takes on the care of a child.

- Group-work, which allows for peer discussion about the issues and self-exploration in a group environment – sometimes known as the educative approach.

- Self-assessment groups, which take this a stage further into peer evaluation.

- Competence / task-centred assessments, which provide a detailed job description of fostering and adoption and measure whether the applicants can demonstrate (with supporting evidence) that, in the here and now, they have the necessary skills (see BAAF Forms as above, Section E). Guidance on how to cross-reference particular skills with both the Children's Workforce Development Council (CWDC) Standards and the BAAF Fostering Competencies is given in Chapman (2009).

- Exploring personal qualities / or "critical capacities". This thematic method looks for evidence that the applicants have the necessary qualities to do the job. These qualities might be: empathy, flexibility, resilience, stability, reliability; a rooted identity; and the capacity to manage "difference", change, dependence, conflict, and co-operation with others. (An exploration of this method for use with second–time adopters is provided by Beesley, 2009.)

What will become obvious in this training film is that there are even more imaginative tools yet to be developed for preparing and assessing applicants, and that demonstrating robust evidence of suitability to adopt or foster, whilst challenging, is not impossible.

Now comes the second element in the assessment trilogy: preparation.

Preparation and learning

It was stated above that the processes of learning and assessment must be combined, and that opportunities should be created where applicants can be educated about the task at the same time as an assessment profile is gradually developed. Some aspects of the models just outlined offer these opportunities, but it is nevertheless very difficult to convey to anxious applicants exactly what may lie ahead. What if the applicants have never cared for a child – or never come across an adopted person? What if they feel scared about taking a child who is disabled? What if they believe that most children who come into care are orphans? Or that birth parents must be inherently bad? Or think that their existing children will warmly welcome a new child into the family? These people should not be dismissed as unsuitable just by virtue of their ignorance – they need to be led to understand and empathise with the reality of children's situations.

Preparation courses are often very imaginative and do this task well, using a combination of input and exercises. Agencies, through openness and good communication, even manage the delicacies of combining an assessment element within the preparation group, where applicants under scrutiny also need to be relaxed enough to concentrate on learning.

But, however good the current system, the mismatch between children who wait and the wishes of applicants means that, at any one time, several hundred children will have been waiting for many months, even years, for a new family. So the real questions are: Can more be done with the applicants at the preparation stage? Can they be taken on a developmental journey which enables them realistically to consider looking at other, different children – maybe a child who is outside their immediate comfort zone? Would this close the gap?

Matching

The final part of this trilogy is the real crunch: how the match is made between children and new families – what influences it, who chooses whom and what factors must be taken into account.

There are some stark facts to be faced. Research has shown that over a quarter of the 3–11–year–olds for whom adoption was in principle agreed were never placed with an adoptive family (Selwyn et al, 2006). If placement disruptions are added, it becomes evident that a significant number of children never achieve adoption, and are at risk of never having a permanent family at all.

Clearly something has to be done to improve this dire situation. As described above, there may be roughly equal numbers of children and new families waiting – but they simply don't match up. The children cannot be changed – so what is it about the family-finding process which could be enhanced so that this dilemma is resolved?

Firstly, a wider and more diverse group of prospective adopters and foster carers could be encouraged to come forward. More black families are certainly needed. Attempts to recruit single, older or disabled people and gay and lesbian couples have been, to some extent, successful. However, the problem for these "minorities" is not in getting past the first hurdle and convincing an adoption panel of their suitability, but at the next stage – in being matched with a child or children. All the old prejudices start to emerge as soon as a child is identified. Social workers responsible for children often have a fairly traditional idea of what constitutes an acceptable family, and tend to be unenthusiastic about exploring minority applicants. This hurdle is huge – but with a wider range of applicants in the pool, the chances of making appropriate matches are almost certain to increase.

The second way the problem could be tackled is to question who is the best party to identify a link – the social worker or the adopters /

foster carers themselves. Some home studies still use hypothetical discussions to determine the kinds of child or children whom the applicants, from the comfort of their armchairs, think they could take. This is written into the assessment report, is often endorsed by panel (erroneously in the case of adoption[2]) and then becomes the basis for the social worker's search for a suitable child. There are several flaws in this: the hypothetical nature of the discussion; the fact that the range of children considered is severely limited by this process; and the way in which, during this paper exercise, children are inevitably reduced to a shortlist of characteristics – a method which is bound to highlight deficits and invoke stereotypes while obscuring the real child. This process is largely controlled by professionals, but if the tables could be turned and if prospective families could see the children (or films of them) and be guided by their intuitive response, unexpected links would emerge. This potential link, generated by adopters and foster carers falling in love with the real child, would then be tested through further specific assessment (Cousins, 2003).

The third way in which progress might be made in placing children is for the adoption journey to become not easier, but even more challenging and experiential. Through testing exercises, such as those described here, applicants can be helped to discover abilities they might not realise they have and, more importantly, they can be drawn into engaging with the reality of the children who need families.

It is understandable that newcomers to the world of public care anxiously stick with what they know but, even without stretching people unrealistically, there are ways to expand applicants' vision, to increase their confidence and ultimately to find families for the most desperate children.

This is what this training film explores.

The assessors

Much has now been said about the applicants and the assessment process – but very little about the assessors themselves: the family placement social workers. Three important issues which need unpicking are: gate-keeping, "gut feelings" and the endemic unwillingness to intrude. A word will also be said about what constitutes observation.

Gate-keeping

Gate-keeping is about social workers controlling the matching process to protect "their" family, rather than putting the needs of children first.

It is very easy for assessors, drawn into applicants' lives during the home study, to collude unconsciously with the family – with the risk that the final goal is not to find the best possible family for a child (who is probably under another team), but to find the least complex child for "their" couple. Family-finders have been known to filter out children *they* regard as unsuitable and thus protect the family from a link that might have worked. Children are the losers.

There is a story of an Exchange Day[3] when a couple (prospective adopters) showed great interest in the profile of a particular child displayed among dozens of others on an agency's table. When they had finally moved on to look at other agencies' tables and profiles, their social worker, who had noted from afar what was happening, approached the first table and enquired who Mr and Mrs X had been interested in. When she was shown the profile of the child and realised that the young person had Down's syndrome, she was crestfallen and asked the agency not to take this any further with her couple. In fact, the anecdote goes, she asked the agency to hide the profile.

This is a shocking (and true) story, but not a million miles from the way some social workers are tempted to screen out children when selecting whom to show to their newly-approved families. Taking control of the process and becoming a (misguided) ambassador for the family rather than an advocate for children allows market forces to prevail over child-centred planning. This is why the most straightforward families will be found the least complex children, while single, older or disabled adopters (all less "desirable") will be offered disabled or highly challenging children even though they may have fewer supports. Unless social workers resist colluding with this topsy-turvy planning, the market-place model will continue. Good supervision is key to tackling this.

The solution is for social workers to relinquish some of their control over the early stages of the matching process and to give more credence to the possibility that adopters and foster carers who are well prepared can make decisions for themselves about a child who would be suitable.

So while the exercises in this film push *applicants* to expand their vision of the kind of child they can take, they also encourage *social workers* to widen their horizons, and believe in the power of applicants' self-awareness, commitment and resilience – and, most of all, to put the needs of children first.

Gut feelings

The second issue is what to do about those "gut feelings". Social workers are so determined to remain non-judgmental that they can end up mistrusting their instincts. How many times among family-finders has the phrase been used: *'I can't really put my finger on it but I've got a gut feeling that there's something not quite right here'*. It would be easy to dismiss these very personal reactions because it is feared they may be judgmental, or they can't be supported with evidence – but assessors do so at their peril.

What is instinct or "gut feeling"? Is it really quite so mysterious? Surely it is nothing more than myriad tiny observations which haven't yet been understood or articulated? The task is

not to ignore it but to interrogate it, and to find evidence which either supports or refutes the emerging hypothesis. Assessors must trust that every little observation counts, even (and maybe most of all) what happens outside the formal assessment process, and could contribute towards evidence.

For example, you can't really picture the applicants being warm and supportive to a child even though they are saying all the right things. So you have a gut feeling that something isn't quite right – but no evidence. Then you realise that on each visit after your long car journey to their home you are not offered a drink on arrival and you have never been shown where the toilet is. What does that tell you? Surely that is a small piece of evidence that perhaps these people are actually reluctant or unable to think of another person's needs? – a new perspective on them which should be tested further: the hypothesis, if you like.

In another case you have the impression that though one partner is very keen on becoming an adopter or foster carer, the other is not – but they are both, on the surface, talking as one. So something feels wrong. Then you realise that all that fiddling with the mobile phone is actually a sign of disengagement – and, added to that, the applicant in question doesn't seem particularly interested in looking at the photographs of the child under consideration. So reading body language is a crucial part of assessment.

Once during an assessment, the male applicant I was interviewing suddenly started to mend a broken living room chair that I knew had been broken for months. It was a bizarre moment. I then realised that the subject under discussion at that point was causing him extreme distress, despite his telling me that he had "got over it all". So his body language, through this extraordinary displacement activity, was alerting me to a sub-text which I had to find ways of exploring further.

The main messages here are:

- think outside the box: allow yourself to be curious about what happens outside the formal assessment sessions;

- take note of everything your antennae are picking up, especially body language;

- respect "gut feelings";

- construct a hypothesis;

- search for relevant evidence – build a picture;

- find ways to tackle the issue from another angle;

- trust your judgment;

- accept that making sound judgments is not the same as being judgmental.

So that is yet another task within the assessment process: to find imaginative ways to explore in greater depth the areas about which, at some subterranean level, there are concerns.

Intrusiveness

The third issue is social workers' fear of being intrusive. Some of the exercises in the training film will almost certainly invoke astonished cries of 'We can't do that to people!' But why not? Someone else's child is, after all, about to be trusted to the care of virtual strangers – so, arguably, no test is a test too far. Readers will remember the quotation from Alyson Leslie's report on the death of the little boy John Anthony in Brighton and Hove when he was placed with adopters:

> *No test is too rigorous and no questioning too intrusive, where the credibility, honesty and reliability of individuals who wish to become adopters are concerned.*
> (Leslie, 2001, p29)

Protecting children therefore has to come first, requiring assessments to be respectful but also robust and investigative. Social workers should never feel embarrassed about challenging potential adopters and foster carers: they may develop a friendly, informal relationship which is supportive and enabling, but they are not the family's friend. Maintaining a professional distance makes it much easier to push and challenge – it is very much more difficult if the prospective carers have arranged work experience for your niece or sold you one of their adorable pedigree puppies.

Lord Laming's phrase 'respectful uncertainty' from the Victoria Climbié inquiry is helpful as a reminder of this balancing act:

> *The concept of "respectful uncertainty" should lie at the heart of the relationship between the social worker and the family. It does not require social workers constantly to interrogate their clients, but it does involve the critical evaluation of information that they are given. People who abuse their children are unlikely to inform social workers of the fact. For this reason at least, social workers must keep an open mind.* (Laming, 2003, p 205, http://publications.everychildmatters.gov.uk/)

Laming is of course talking about families in the community, but this advice is equally applicable to the assessment of prospective adopters and foster carers.

However, although there is a clear rationale for rigorous enquiry, the only legitimate basis for investigation is around the needs of children – and the qualities and abilities of the family to do the task. Social workers are not there to make judgments about anything else.

Observation

Much has been said above about the need to observe the minutiae of people's behaviour during the assessment process. To some extent this is a covert operation, even if the observations are subsequently shared with the applicants.

Later in this workbook, however, allusion is briefly made to "fly-on-the-wall" observation. This is where the assessor openly arranges to watch a prospective adopter or foster carer managing a particular activity – possibly a children's tea party or a "borrowed" child's visit to their home. In this case, the assessor plays no part at all in the proceedings and remains as neutral as possible, much as a researcher might, making notes where necessary. This is quite hard to achieve, but it does provide an opportunity to concentrate on the interactions between the key players.

The training film

Introduction

As described above, the aim of the training film, *Preparing Families*, is to showcase new training techniques and exercises which encourage adopters and foster carers to consider children for whom it is hard to find families, by:

- providing more information about these children;

- offering hands-on care opportunities;

- boosting the applicants' confidence so they realise they could cope with children they might not previously have considered.

Viewers will also see that some of the exercises are designed to "surprise the unconscious" and help both assessor and assessed to understand more about how the applicant might function when caring for a wider variety of children. The exercises therefore offer opportunities to complement and extend the more usual models of assessment.

The prospective adopters in the film series engaged in a three-stage process:

- a residential weekend which used exercises to understand their motivation for adopting, to test their relationship dynamics and to get a feel for the kind of children they thought they could cope with.

- a weekend in their own home with a "borrowed" child to give them hands-on

experience. A child was chosen who would really stretch their ideas of what they thought they could cope with.

- once the adopters became clearer about the kind of child they could take or when a possible link was on the horizon, any particular concerns they had were tackled through arranging visits to special schools and youth groups. In these settings, specific questions could be answered, and the adopters were helped to feel more confident about considering a real child.

It was readily acknowledged earlier that some of the exercises are ambitious – but the film and this workbook offer ideas about how to use them to fit with the resources available. Hopefully they will inspire many more adaptations than the limited range suggested here.

Format

David Akinsanya introduces the film and takes the viewer through each chapter. David is an adoption and fostering campaigner and the presenter for the TV series. You will gradually meet four different sets of prospective adopters:

- Rachel – a single white woman of 34 and her brother (her supporter, not himself an adopter);

- John and Anthony – two gay white men in their forties/fifties;

- Suma and Albert – a black couple in their thirties and their children;

- Cathy and Richard – a white couple in their thirties and their eight–year–old birth daughter.

You will also meet Teresa, social worker for Rachel; Rebecca, social worker for John and Anthony; and Stephen, the psychologist for the series. Some of the quotations from the film which are used in the workbook have been edited.

Following the introduction, the film is divided into five chapters exploring different exercises:

1   Introduction

2   Case study exercise

3   Teenage adoption panel

4   Under pressure exercise

5   Trial parenting exercise

6   Tailor-made experiences

In each film chapter you will see the exercise in practice, hear the social worker's comments and the psychologist's observations.

The workbook

This workbook follows Chapters 2–6, each of which is a self-contained unit to be used as flexibly as desired. It is suggested that you watch each short film chapter where indicated in the text.

You will be introduced to the aim of the exercise and prepared for what you will see in the film chapter. Then you will be given suggested learning points, which can be expanded upon in team discussion. Next comes a section, *Into Practice*, on how to prepare and run the exercise, and a list of alternative exercises, or variants, which it is hoped might also fulfil the desired aims, or expand the possibilities even further. Readers are then reminded of the learning points in a summary.

The final two sections of each chapter are in the form of a notebook, the first of which, *Notes on the assessment task,* is to aid the job of drawing together assessment material, and report-writing. The reports are the Prospective Adopter's Report and the BAAF Form F (Fostering) – or Prospective Foster Carer(s) Report. Having explored all (relevant) aspects of the applicant's life, assessors are required to provide evidence of "suitability" – namely that the prospective adopter or foster carer is suitable to fulfil that complex and demanding role. The social worker faced with this

challenging task may find the following three questions helpful:

1   How can this exercise be used to open up certain issues for further exploration?

2   What evidence might emerge from this exercise about some of the skills and qualities necessary to become an adopter or foster carer?

3   Does this exercise provide any specific evidence needed in order to arrive at a recommendation about this applicant?

This third question is designed to prompt assessors to think about any missing evidence which might be found here, or to act as a reminder to delve into areas where there are still concerns.

The final notebook section, *Prompts for in-house discussion*, is intended to stimulate agency debate about exploring organisational constraints, seeking solutions, and launching some of the new techniques.

Notes

1   The terms "BAAF Form F (Fostering)" and "Prospective Adopter's Report" are used here for simplicity. In fact, there are now assessment forms covering adoption, fostering and permanent fostering to suit the separate needs of England, Wales, Scotland and Northern Ireland. Because of the relative size of the countries, the most common adoption report is the Prospective Adopter's Report (known as the PAR) – one for England and one for Wales. In Scotland and Northern Ireland, it is the Form F Adoption and Permanence (country-specific). Most of the fostering reports are known as Form F Fostering (country-specific).

2   An adoption panel *may* give advice about the 'number, age range, sex, likely needs and background' of the child/children it considers would be appropriate for the prospective adopters… 'but the agency is not restricted by such advice' (Adoption

and Children Act 2002, Statutory Guidance, Chapter 3, paragraph 60). It is important that agencies appreciate that this advice does not constitute a formal recommendation, and that a match with any child may subsequently be proposed without returning to panel for a 'change of approval' which (erroneously) was thought to be required under the previous legislation.

3   Exchange Days take place across the country in large venues like community centres or town halls. A number of adoption agencies attend, representing the children in their area who are waiting for families. Wall-boards show photographs of the children, plus information and sometimes children's artwork and a short video. Flyers are available to take away. Approved adopters are invited and have the opportunity to browse the material and talk directly to the children's social workers.

Chapter 2
Case study exercise

Introduction

It may seem very obvious to assessors and trainers that discussing case studies is a helpful exercise, but here the method has been developed further to serve a number of purposes. The case studies used in the film are anonymised versions of real children although, because of the wider circulation, those at the back of this workbook have been further fictionalised.

Aim of the exercise

The aim is to get applicants to think about the children who need families and to consider those they could parent – and those they could not. This may be the first time the applicants have had to face these questions and they need the opportunity to explore this for themselves.

The case studies are neutral in terms of "race" and culture. There is a reason for this. The aim is to introduce families to a full range of children and their previous experiences, and to tap into the applicants' responses. Were the child's racial heritage or ethnicity to be signalled, this could divert the exercise solely onto the question of ethnic matching, which should be given its own due space at a later point in the process.

The film

What you will see

What you see in the film is prospective adopters evaluating a series of case studies privately in pairs. You will meet John and Anthony (partners) and Rachel (a single applicant) and her brother; also Teresa, who is Rachel's social worker, and Stephen, the film's psychologist.

Now watch the film

Learning points

This exercise provides an opportunity for adopters to begin to explore the kinds of children who need new families – a reality check, if you like. It is evident that the adopters in the film are at the very beginning of the learning process as their responses are sympathetic, but a little naive.

1   Observing this exercise would provide social workers with useful base-line data on which to build an assessment, including evidence about the adopters' knowledge, communication styles, and some aspects of their relationship, for example, whether they listen appropriately or acknowledge the other person's concerns and so on. In the film, John and Anthony readily tune into each other's point of view.

2   As mentioned above, these are cases of real children. This has a huge impact and it is certainly recommended that real cases

are used (with the usual safeguards), and that people are told this. No one can dodge the reality of children's lives or think that social workers might be exaggerating. However, there is a risk that, without support, the applicants may be so overwhelmed by children's experiences that they are alienated from the whole process.

3   It is also clear that these adopters do not understand the range of behaviours which some of the terms cover, and are writing off a child before considering that there will be many individual variations within each term (for example, autistic spectrum disorder; attachment difficulties) which could be manageable. All this is entirely natural at this very early stage but demonstrates the risks if social workers give too much weight to these initial responses.

4   What you also see in the film is the adopters struggling to deal with the experiences children have lived through: they are overwhelmed and upset by what they read. John says:

You can't imagine what these children have been through. When you read that children have been begging for food from neighbours…blisters caused by urine…little girl – strangulation marks round her throat…

In these situations adopters need to understand that their shock and revulsion at what happens to children – and anger towards the perpetrators – is a legitimate response that can be discussed at length later in the process.

5   The other striking feature is the guilt which the adopters feel about allocating a case study to the "Won't accept" pile and symbolically rejecting children. Rachel begins to weep when her brother says:

I hope there are people out there who can take these kids and not do what we're doing and kind of tossing them to one side.

Anthony says:

Do you know – it makes me feel…oh god – GUILTY! – because I am turning people down and I don't want to turn people down…You do want to grab the whole lot…you really do.

Adopters will need reassurance about this. Unless the guilty feelings are aired and acknowledged to be normal, adopters later in the process may overcompensate by saying they could take a child who would in fact stretch them too far. Although feeling very guilty, Anthony takes a rational view and says, '*You can't give a home to all the children but it has to be the right child*', and it is true that, if a match is not right for the adopters, it will not be right for the child. So this exercise gives opportunities to stretch people's imagination but also gives them permission to keep a foothold in reality.

Just a note of warning: as mentioned above, the point where this case study exercise is used in the film would be very early days to be actually ruling out whole groups of children – it is exploratory only.

6   It is valuable for a single applicant to have a supporter with them. In Rachel's case it also gives her brother a real idea of what his sister is about to take on. Rachel says to him: '*I think that probably for the first time you understand a bit more about what I want to do.*' Stephen, the psychologist, comments:

This is a simple, painless, non-intrusive way of introducing wider family to some of the implications of taking on a child who may come with a particular package of difficulties…because it's not just the adopters themselves who are going to be left dealing with the potential problems that a child may come with.

7   It is also useful to get the supporter's own views about the applicant. Here, Rachel's brother, in a caring way, asks whether she is really "patient" enough and raises

questions about her poor level of self-confidence. He says:

When you have your little "down moments" and not feeling very confident about yourself – I'm just worried that a kid with low self-esteem might pick up on that.

Stephen, the psychologist, comments:

Somebody from the extended family can often offer a perspective on the adopter that might otherwise be missed – they often know them very well – they know their strengths, their weaknesses…and that conversation would be a really helpful source of information for social workers.

Into practice

Method

There are three master cards (*Will accept, Won't accept, Not sure*) and about ten case studies. The master cards are laid out so that three separate piles can be created.

Ask the participants to consider the child on each case study one by one and discuss with their partner whether they could imagine realistically taking on the care of that child. Then they will place that card on one of the piles to indicate their decision.

Ask them (in couples) to look at the finished piles and talk with each other about their thoughts and feelings. This is shared (either simultaneously or later) with the assessing social worker and a discussion follows.

Although questions of "matching" will arise, keep the discussion open at this point rather than allowing it to become prescriptive.

Materials

You may use the case studies in this workbook (see Chapter 8) or devise your own.

Paste a brief profile of a child (or a sibling group) onto a card, which should then ideally be laminated. Make about ten of these profile cards.

Make three master cards:

- Will accept
- Won't accept
- Not sure

It is important that all these cards look professional and are carefully and respectfully produced. Their quality should mirror the respect which should be shown to the children and to the prospective adopters.

If you wish to add even greater potential to this case study exercise, create a second set of profile cards giving more information about each child.

Preparing the exercise

If making your own case studies, review the children in care in your agency and choose a selection (about ten) demonstrating a range of ages, background circumstances, difficulties, impairments, sibling situation and so on.

Condense each child's details into a brief profile of no more than one side of A4 (or about 250 words). Make sure that you change names and any identifying information.

At the beginning of the exercise, say that although the material has been anonymised, the children in these case studies are real children in real situations and that you are aware that their profiles can be quite distressing to read and think about. Explain why at this point you have not noted the child's ethnicity (see above, under *Aim of the exercise*).

Alternative exercises

There are many different ways of using case studies. Some of these extra ideas are described by the social worker Teresa and the psychologist Stephen during the film.

1   As suggested above, observe the couple (or single applicant and friend/supporter) doing the exercise together without your intervention.

2   Tailor the cards for each couple to open up a discussion about particular kinds of children. This will test the water by raising ideas of children outside the adopters' apparent comfort zone and demonstrate where the limits might be for that individual or couple.

3   Now is the time to open up the debate about "race" and ethnicity. Either use a new set, or reissue the cards, this time with an additional sticker giving the child's racial and cultural background. These should reflect the community where your service is located. Even in predominantly white areas it would be important to include children of other racial, cultural and ethnic backgrounds so that these issues can be fully explored.

4   As an assessing social worker, tailor the cards to raise particular issues and questions which are already forming in the back of your mind about the adopters.

5   Provide a spectrum of scenarios within a particular area of difficulty/disability so that adopters, instead of ruling out all children with that label, might be prepared to accept someone at the easier or milder end of that spectrum.

6   Ask the couple to read and allocate the cards individually – then discuss with each other and with the assessor to see if there are any discrepancies and what issues have emerged.

7   Ask them to repeat the exercise some weeks later and discuss any differences or movement from the first time.

8   Using the second set of cards which contain more information about each child, ask the adopters to repeat the exercise (either individually or as a couple, or both) and discuss.

9   Ask them to do the exercise as if they were a particular member of the extended family evaluating them (e.g. one of their own parents or a sibling); then go to the family member and see how their response chimes with that of the adopters.

10 Ask the prospective adopters to discuss the case study child in relation to the dimensions of the *Assessment Framework* (child's developmental needs; family and environmental factors and parenting capacity) and discuss the issues which emerge.

11 Ask the couple to think about the local services and resources which they would have to call upon if that child were placed with them. This could be done as homework so that some real investigation could take place around each case study child – for example, the location of a pharmacy, GP practice, speech therapy centre, toddler group, hearing clinic, hospital Accident & Emergency department, park with swings.

12 Think about adapting the exercise to a group preparation setting. However, if you are doing this in a group, reassure participants that, as with all exercises, they can take "time out" if it raises difficult issues for them.

13 Set up a special information event for family, friends and supporters, using case studies. This will enable everyone in the adopters' support network to get a feeling for what is involved. As Stephen, the psychologist says: *'It takes a village to raise a child – but the village needs to be aware of what it's in for!'*

14 Extend the exercise by using photographs of children to represent each case study text. There could be many variants to this, but one suggestion is as follows. Give all the photographs to the applicant and ask them to allocate each to a pile: *Will accept, Won't accept, Not sure.* Then repeat the exercise using the texts only. Then check to see if the photographs and the texts of

each child have been put on the same pile. Discuss how people feel about their choices and about the reunited profiles. Discuss the power of photographs; and that although an immediate response to how a child looks is very important, adopters must also think about a child's personality and history in order to make an informed decision. Photographs of "models" are provided in the back of this workbook, which can be colour-photocopied.

15 Another variation can be devised in order to challenge some of the stereotypes that prevent children being placed. For example, if the words "cerebral palsy" are flagged up, many people would automatically put this child on the "Won't accept" pile, but they might think it would be relatively easy to take a child with "attachment difficulties".

Make up two case studies: Child A, a well-nurtured child who has cerebral palsy (but do not indicate the disability – just describe other things about the child); the second, Child B, who has been badly neglected and shows a degree of complex behaviour.

Ask the applicants to say how confident they would feel about caring for each child. Many people will think that Child A would be easier to care for. When the applicants have made their assessment and are told that Child A has cerebral palsy and Child B has an attachment difficulty, they are often surprised at how misunderstood a label can be.

16 Ask the adopters (both those with existing children *and* those who are childless) to think again about the case studies with the idea that this is a child who is joining a family who already have children. What would the impact be? Where would the tensions and stresses arise? This would work well as a group discussion.

Summary of learning points

→ Real case studies are the most powerful. Make sure that the child or family is not identifiable.

→ Applicants' initial assessments of what they can and can't deal with are just that – initial. It would be unwise to give too much weight to them.

→ Applicants may need reassurance that their responses to children's histories and experiences are normal.

→ Acknowledge the guilt that people feel at "rejecting" children.

→ Single applicants can be invited to do this exercise with a supporter.

→ Check that it's OK to use the supporter's opinions in future discussions.

Notes on the assessment task: case study exercise

It is suggested that when working with applicants, assessors should use the exercise (or a variant) outlined in each chapter and then, using a photocopied version of this worksheet (which is chapter-specific), reflect on the issues raised by the exercise for the assessment of this particular applicant / couple, and the evidence of suitability it may provide.

1. **How can this exercise be used to open up certain issues for further exploration? It may provide opportunities to explore:**

→ The reality of children's lives; the emotions evoked.

_____

_____

→ Expectations about the "kind of child" who is available and also whom the applicants could envisage taking.

_____

_____

→ The policy and practice issue of transracial and transcultural placements.

_____

_____

→ Any differences of opinion or attitude between the partners.

_____

_____

→ Lifestyle changes if this child were to join the family.

_____

_____

→ The impact on other family members, including existing children.

_____

_____

→ The suitability of the neighbourhood and environment.

_____

_____

→ That each child is an individual; that for each type of behaviour / disability / medical condition there is a wide spectrum of severity.

_____

_____

→ The implications of a respect for confidentiality and individual dignity.

_____

_____

→ The life-long nature of adoption and the supports necessary / available.

_____

_____

2. **What evidence might emerge from this exercise about some of the skills and qualities necessary to become an adopter or foster carer, which can be used in the assessment report?**

    The case study exercise may provide direct evidence about the applicant's:

    → Current knowledge about the nature of the task ahead (and, when repeated, how that knowledge has increased during the assessment period).

    _____

    _____

    → Individual and shared motivation to adopt/foster and any discrepancies between partners.

    _____

    _____

    → Understanding of their own strengths and vulnerabilities.

    _____

    _____

    → Attitudes to diversity: intrinsic as well as background issues (including attitudes to the birth family's lifestyle).

    _____

    _____

    → Present knowledge of child development and the impact of trauma.

    _____

    _____

3. **Assessor's self-check: does this exercise provide any specific evidence I need in order to come to a recommendation about this applicant?**

    _____

    _____

Prompts for in-house discussion: case study exercise

This worksheet (which is chapter-specific) can be photocopied and used in a team meeting or other agency forum to stimulate discussion about the exercise and how it may be applied.

• Can you identify enough children to use as examples in a case study exercise? If not, what will you do?

_____

_____

• Would you use it in a home study assessment or part of group preparation?

_____

_____

• Which form/s of the exercise would particularly suit your purposes?

_____

_____

• Would there be any barriers to setting this up? If so, how could you overcome them?

_____

_____

• Are there any cultural considerations to be taken into account?

_____

_____

Chapter 3
Teenage adoption panel

Introduction

This exercise brings adopters face to face with a panel of adopted young people and their experiences. The teenagers' personal insights have helped them to construct questions that really challenge the adopters. It is also striking that the usual power relationship between adults and children has been switched: here the young people are in charge. Stephen, the psychologist, says:

This was amongst the most useful and transformative things that the adopters did during the process.

Aim of the exercise

The aim is to explore more about the adopters' motivation and how their understanding of adoption is evolving through the process.

The film

What you will see

What you will see is a group of six adopted young people who have prepared questions to ask the adopters – in the style of an adoption panel. The adopters are interviewed in turn. There are pauses in the film so that you can stop to reflect after each question is posed.

The teenagers' questions are as follows:

1   How do you think adoption will affect the life you have already?

2   How do you think your birth children are going to cope with having an adopted brother or sister?

3   What drawbacks do you think there are to being a gay couple? How are you going to deal with it if the child does start to get bullied?

4   Could you deal with and understand why an adopted child might display extreme attention-seeking behaviour or really bad behaviour that was very difficult to cope with?

5   If in a couple of years' time the adopted child started to influence your children to do bad things – getting into trouble, running away all the time, getting brought back by the police – do you think you'd be able to put up with that and not have to go back to social services and ask for help?

You will also note two personal anecdotes from the young people: one about being bullied because of being adopted, and the other about being returned to care by adoptive parents.

You will notice that the panel seems to be composed of young white people who do not have disabilities. In setting up such a panel it would be very important to aim to appoint a more representative cross section of the community to include BME and disabled young people.

As well as the young people, you will meet prospective adopters Cathy and Richard, Suma and Albert, John and Anthony, and Rachel. You will also hear from Stephen the psychologist and Teresa, Rachel's social worker.

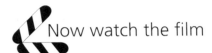

Now watch the film

Learning points

1   This live exercise is only a snapshot but it reveals quite a lot about the adopters' views and attitudes, including how they relate to a young person. It is important that the social worker is present during this panel interview to observe as well as support.

In this film clip, the adopters' respect for the young people is evident, both during the interview and in the subsequent debriefing. They treat the occasion with the solemnity it deserves and are clearly challenged by the questions.

2   The film also demonstrates that these are questions – all absolutely central to the adoption task – that will need more exploration during the home study. For example:

• Cathy shows that her main consideration is the impact on their daughter Rachel – a realistic preoccupation that will undoubtedly be picked up in the home study. However, in the film clip, they do not really describe how their lifestyle would change with a new family member – which it most certainly will.

• Suma and Albert have clearly been preparing their family through books and general discussions about children who 'have never had love' and say their children are excited about the prospect of adoption. Later, in response to the last question, they express absolute determination to stick with a child who has gone off the rails, valuing and loving the new child as their own. Their responses are naïve but very touching. However, the questions will give them food for thought and provide a basis for discussion with their social worker.

• John and Anthony home straight in on the disadvantage in the school environment to a prospective child who is placed with them as a gay couple. They provide examples of the ways they would actually handle this, though for the Prospective Adopter's Report they will need to be more explicit about the "strategies" they say they would offer the child.

• Rachel struggles a bit to articulate her thoughts, but does equate early lack of love and attention with later behavioural difficulties – again an issue that will need more elaboration with her social worker.

3   The debriefing session afterwards is important in providing the social worker with further evidence of how the adopters are progressing on their journey towards understanding adoption and all its life-long implications. Meeting adopted children from a variety of backgrounds who have become responsible young adults can have a significant impact on adopters. Their reactions should be captured as soon as possible after the event. Again, these are issues for the home study.

4   A key point is that these are questions which the young people themselves have identified as important, and therefore the questions have legitimacy and urgency. The young people raise real-life situations and ask 'what would you do?' Teresa says that the exercise had a big impact on Rachel because:

This wasn't a profile – it was somebody who had been through a particular experience saying 'how would you have dealt with this had I been your child?'

Rachel confirms this:

It's a really good exercise – to put yourself in their shoes and try and understand some of the things they have come across and the problems they've had... they can really challenge you as to how would you deal with that situation.

5   Unlike the home study, when these questions are explored through artificial exercises, this time real emotions are involved. Albert, the prospective adopter, says:

It was absolutely fantastic. This is about real life – I was really moved emotionally to see these children asking questions – they're not just questions on paper – it's about the experiences they've been through – it's really touching.

6   A further point is that the young people themselves hold the power in this exercise. There is no explicit discussion about this in the film, but the issues of adult power and respect for children should be raised with prospective adopters.

7   The adopters learn that young people who have been adopted are "quite normal". This may be contrary to some of the fears and stereotypes harboured by adopters who have been overwhelmed by accounts of horrific childhoods. Teresa, Rachel's social worker, says that these were *...young people they could bump into in a shop but they've been through all these different issues and actually they've turned out OK.*

8   The added value of meeting adopted young adults is for adopters to realise that adopted babies and small children grow up still carrying the marks of their history. This is a reminder that adoption is a life-long experience.

9   The teenage panel interview is also a "stress test" (explored in the next chapter). It puts people on the spot and can reveal basic characteristics, underlying attitudes, relationship dynamics and preoccupations. From these very small clips we can see how Cathy's main concern pops to the surface (her daughter); how John willingly takes a secondary place to Anthony who is more experienced at such meetings – but remains 100% engaged; and how Rachel under pressure does not think as clearly as usual. These observations in themselves do not lead to conclusions about people, but do offer small pieces of evidence which can be tested further.

Into practice

Method

For those with experience of adoption and fostering panels, the method is self-explanatory. Select a group of young adopted people, decide on questions and an agenda, and invite the adopter/s in to be interviewed. After each session, allow time for the young people to debrief amongst themselves. Notes may be taken of these discussions.

As mentioned above, it is important to select a wide range of young people including disabled young people and those with a black or minority ethnic background.

Materials

Make sure that the setting is formal, with a boardroom table and the usual props such as water, paper and pens, etc. The setting should convey the seriousness of the occasion.

Preparing the exercise

Given the very delicate nature of the panel's discussion, ensure that all parties are well prepared for the format and the content of the panel meeting.

Preparing the young people

Individual support will be needed for each young person as the exercise is likely to trigger memories of difficult early experiences. A supportive group should be established with a responsible adult in charge, who will later chair the panel.

In this group setting, give a brief outline of each couple / single applicant to the young people, and ask what questions they think are the most relevant to raise during each interview. It is likely that some questions will be appropriate for all applicants while some may need to be more specific – for example, for those who already have children; or are gay / lesbian; or are applying as a single person (as in the film); or are disabled. Agree the wording of the questions, and agree which one each young person will ask. Decide whether to allow for follow-up questions and how these will be handled.

In the film, the Chair is taken by David Akinsanya. It is essential that the person who has done the preparatory work with the group of young people becomes the Chair.

A debriefing session after each interview might be useful (not seen in the film) – but if so, decide what to do with the young people's feedback. If it is to be conveyed to the applicant's social worker, this should be made clear to all parties beforehand.

Preparing the adopters

Young people who are selected to make an important contribution to an event such as a panel are likely to feel valued and important. Adopters must understand and respect this.

Adopters are likely to be nervous about this exercise, as they will have to think on their feet and respond appropriately to the questions. They also know it will feel like a rehearsal for the adoption panel.

The social worker for the applicants will accompany them for support and observation. These observations will be discussed with the applicants afterwards, plus any agreed debriefing notes from the young people themselves. All this is made clear to the adopters in advance. As with all other observations during the period between applying and being approved, adopters need to know how the information will be used. Normally this is fed back in an open way and acknowledged to be part of the assessment of suitability.

Alternative exercises

Although what you see in the film is ideal, it is unlikely that an agency will be able to assemble a group of young adopted people for each

cohort of adopters who are going through the preparation process. However, as Stephen the psychologist says:

> It would be really valuable if it could be replicated more widely even if it's not possible to assemble a group of adopted teens. Even if potential adopters have the chance to talk to one or two young people about their experiences, this would be invaluable.

If you set up an alternative format, you can base it around questions 1–5 (given above) posed by the young people here. With minor amendments, many of the questions can be asked of all applicants.

Some suggested variants are given below. However, whichever method is used, try to include disabled young people and those with a black and minority ethnic background. This should be more than just tokenistic.

1   Find at least two young adopted people who are willing to help in this way in a live panel – or older adopted people with suitable histories. Adult adoptees who have used the birth records counselling service would be a valuable addition.

2   With the usual agreements, film one live session and use it with subsequent preparation groups.

3   Assemble and prepare young people for a one-off video where they each ask their question to camera. Each cohort of adopters can be invited to respond as if it were a live exercise.

4   Using the original format, add a feedback session where the young people relay their observations to the applicant and their social worker so that relevant issues can be taken forward during the assessment.

5   If adopted young people cannot be involved, consider setting up a panel of approved adopters and / or adopters with children already placed – and repeating the exercise. Again, the panel could give feedback to the applicants and their social worker.

6   Show this professionally produced training film during preparation groups, using the pauses (elongated) for group discussion.

7   Use the film to prompt discussion between assessors and adopters during the home study – for example, 'what would you have replied to the teenagers' questions?' and 'what do you think about the filmed answers?'

8   Assemble a range of adopted children willing to talk about adoption, and film their individual or group discussion. By doing this you will be bringing the voice of the child into your preparation process.

9   Using a copy of *Adopted Children Speaking* (Thomas and Beckford, 1999) or *The Colours in Me* (Harris, 2008), read out some of the children's actual quotations to a group of adopters. Even more effective, ask a young person to read these and perhaps give their own thoughts.

10 Turn the original exercise round so that an audience of adopters asks questions of a panel of adoption experts (like the TV programme *Question Time*). The experts would include at least two young adopted people, a selection of adopters and two social workers. Assessors would observe the exercise and debrief their family afterwards.

Summary of learning points

→ This exercise provides an opportunity for the assessing social worker to observe the adopters dealing with a stressful situation, and to see what views and attitudes emerge under this pressure.

→ The panel gives an opportunity to gauge where the adopters are up to in their thinking about adoption. Issues are likely to emerge which will provide material for further discussion in the home study.

→ This format – using young adopted people themselves – is the most powerful. Adopters' understanding of a range of adoption-related issues is considerably extended because of the emotional component.

→ Two advantages which are not replicable using other methods are that this teenage panel demonstrates that adopted children can grow up to function like any other adult, and that adopters need to focus on life-long issues, not just the here and now of placement.

Notes on the assessment task: teenage adoption panel

It is suggested that when working with applicants, assessors should use the exercise (or a variant) outlined in each chapter and then, using a photocopied version of this worksheet (which is chapter-specific), reflect on the issues raised by the exercise for the assessment of this particular applicant / couple, and the evidence of suitability it may provide.

1. **How can this exercise be used to open up certain issues for further exploration? It may provide opportunities to explore:**

→ The motivation of the applicants in wanting to adopt or foster.

_____

_____

→ The applicants' expectations and whether these are realistic.

_____

_____

→ The emotional impact of hearing real questions arising from young people's experiences.

_____

_____

→ The power balance between adults and adolescents, and what it feels like when a young person is in control asking questions.

_____

_____

→ The life-long nature of adoption and the supports necessary / available.

_____

_____

→ The *Question Time* variation would provide further discussion material about power relationships and children's rights.

_____

2. **What evidence might emerge from this exercise about some of the skills and qualities necessary to become an adopter or foster carer, which can be used in the assessment report?**

   The teenage panel exercise (including the *Question Time* variation) may provide direct evidence about:

   → The applicants' attitudes to young people.

   _____

   _____

   → Their ability to communicate appropriately in framing sensitive questions and listening respectfully.

   _____

   _____

   → Their ability to advocate on their own behalf.

   _____

   _____

   → Their attitude to diversity, especially if the panel is of mixed ethnicity and disability.

   _____

   _____

   → The dynamics of the couple's relationship.

   _____

   _____

   → How applicants react under stress.

   _____

   _____

3. **Assessor's self-check: does this exercise provide any specific evidence I need in order to come to a recommendation about this applicant?**

   _____

   _____

Prompts for in-house discussion: teenage adoption panel

This worksheet (which is chapter-specific) can be photocopied and used in a team meeting or other agency forum to stimulate discussion about the exercise and how it may be applied.

- Identify any logistical difficulties in setting up this teenage panel exercise and discuss what you can do to overcome them.

_____

_____

- Which feasible alternative would fulfil the same aims?

_____

_____

- How does your agency currently incorporate the perspective of young adopted people for the benefit of those going through the adoption process?

_____

_____

- Does this include children from a wide range of backgrounds and disabled children? If not, what can you do to address this?

_____

_____

- Do you involve adopted adults? If not, how can you now do this?

_____

_____

- Are there any cultural considerations to be taken into account?

_____

_____

Chapter 4
Under pressure exercise

Introduction

In this chapter of the film, Rebecca, the social worker, says: *'Normally our assessment is based on discussions in their living room'*. In the relatively relaxed setting of the applicants' home, the exploration tends to focus on hypothetical situations where people can show themselves to advantage.

However, it was discussed in the introduction to this workbook that the real way to find out how someone ticks is to "surprise the unconscious". That is, to put them under the kind of pressure which does not allow time for a considered response, but taps into a deeper level of their personality – the automatic or spontaneous reactions, shaped by childhood, which are not within conscious control.

It is axiomatic that the advent of a stranger into the family brings not only logistical challenges, but also a psychic upheaval for all members. When this person is a child who is confused, grieving and angry, and maybe, as a way of coping, needs to control their new environment, this upheaval can cause all family members varying degrees of stress.

Aim of the exercise

The aim of this exercise is to see how the adopters operate under pressure – to delve into this instinctual level of an individual's functioning and see how he/she reacts and interacts when high levels of stress strip away the usual social veneer. The exercise would be used to illuminate aspects of the adopter's personality; it would not be used to rule them out *per se*.

The film

What you will see

You will see two different "stress" exercises, both of which aim to replicate aspects of the pressure that a new child entering the family will inevitably cause.

Exercise 1

Suma and Albert are required to put up a tent in only 20 minutes, with no instructions.

The exercise symbolically replicates the stress of taking a child into the family – particularly a child who brings many difficult and unresolved issues of their own. In order to be able to parent such a child effectively, you have to be able to:

- think on your feet

- problem-solve

- stick together and collaborate.

The exercise therefore exposes whether they can achieve this when they are under pressure. The psychologist says:

> *The way that people deal with conflict gives you a lot of insight into the strengths and relative weaknesses of their relationship – and their style of relating.*

Exercise 2

In the second exercise, Rachel is asked to communicate for 20 minutes about a short list of topics, with a woman who speaks no English. The exercise shows how Rachel operates in a stressful situation and it also raises important issues about skills in communication, which is the cornerstone of caring for displaced children.

You will hear from Stephen, the film's psychologist, and Teresa, Rachel's social worker. Rebecca also contributes.

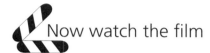

Now watch the film

Learning points

1 The success of this exercise will depend upon social workers feeling comfortable about using stress as a legitimate assessment tool.

   Stephen comments that exercises like these where there is pressure – and especially if there's a time limit – can be quite brutal in what they expose:

   Often when people are under pressure they default to quite regressive child-like patterns of behaviour, so it's worth watching out for the whole interplay of parent / adult / child roles – who does what. If someone is in a parent role, what kind of parent role are they playing? Are they authoritarian and directive, or are they permissive and "anything goes"?

   It can also show very clearly the sort of dynamics that operate between a couple or within a family that might cause difficulties for an adopted child coming into that system.

2 In order to gain everyone's co-operation, it will be important to establish some ground rules (see below, *Preparing the exercise*). Applicants need to trust that what emerges will not be used to eject them from the adoption process: it is purely exploratory. It should also be acknowledged that not everyone performs well under observation.

3 Assessors need to know how a relationship works under pressure. Suma and Albert really struggle with the camping task but Albert tries to make his wife's plan work.

The couple show a high level of what psychologists call "agreeableness" – a desire for things to be harmonious, which can be a real strength. However, the situation might arise where the challenge persists and a solution seems unattainable. In these circumstances, the relationship will be under even greater pressure and more of each person's underlying personality style will be revealed.

Rebecca, the social worker, says:

This exercise was really useful for me to see couples working together – to look at their relationship, their roles, how they deal with problems and to give us an indication of how they might cope once a child is with them.

4 Perhaps one person has to take a definitive lead according to their particular strengths or talents – in which case it will be seen whether the partner is supportive or not.

5 When assessing a single person, this pressure exercise, or a variant, reveals how that person conducts themself under stress: what do they actually do and say? Do they panic or manage calmly? Can they use humour appropriately, laugh at themselves and cope with the exposure which comes from looking foolish? Do they react creatively or inflexibly? Will they struggle on stoically or seek appropriate help and receive it graciously?

6 How a person manages the need to depend on others is a vital assessment issue especially when considering adoption support and, in foster care, the ongoing relationship with the agency. People may regard independence as a strength, whereas in this context it can become a negative, even risky, factor.

7 Effective communication requires particular *skills*.

   Many children will be silenced through trauma, disability or previous neglect; English may not be their most familiar language; and their life experiences may have been very different from those of the adopters.

This exercise, involving the prospective adopter Rachel and a woman who does not speak English, replicates to some extent the issues which face adopters who are trying to relate to a looked after child. Rachel copes very well under the pressure to communicate the *substance* of what she has been asked to talk about – speaking slowly, keeping good eye contact and using creative physical gestures. Stephen, the psychologist, says, '*Research shows that for communicative effectiveness, 93 per cent is down to non-verbal factors*'. Taking English out of the equation emphasises the importance of non-verbal communication and this is a useful lesson for adopters.

Rachel is seen to take responsibility for making the communication run as smoothly as possible, which is vital when working with children. Where there is a communication or language barrier of any kind, it is not the child's responsibility to make it work. Rachel remains calm under pressure and is not fazed by realising she must look foolish – rather, she keeps her focus on the task.

8   Effective communication also requires particular *qualities*.

In this film clip Rachel is seen to maintain rapport even when stressed. Over and above the substance of the issues she is required to explore, she conveys through her smiles, eye contact and body language a real desire to make contact and to be friendly. This is valuable evidence of warmth of personality that is so crucial for children. She also demonstrates inventiveness and patience – a quality you may remember her brother expresses doubt about in the first exercise. Building up communication pathways with a child is an individual process that takes patience and time – another useful lesson. The qualities Rachel displays will be extremely important in welcoming a new child who may not at first respond.

9   An exercise involving uncertainty and vulnerability has an additional purpose. It gives adopters an insight into the feelings of vulnerability that a new child in the family might experience. The adopters could be asked to write about their feelings during this exercise for the home study report and as a basis for discussion.

Into practice

Method

The adopters are asked to do a stressful exercise in a limited amount of time. Discuss what makes them feel uncomfortable and stressed – or start with some ideas of your own and discover their fears / phobias / uncertainties. You then have something on which to base your choice of stressful situations.

In the tent exercise you will notice that Suma says she has never put up a tent before, which is of course why, for her and Albert, this exercise is stressful. However, for a seasoned camper this would be easy. You therefore need to find situations that are genuinely difficult for the people involved.

You can increase the pressure by "fixing" the exercise so it won't work. For example, in the tent exercise, unbeknown to Suma and Albert, there were some poles missing.

Make a video of the exercise and play this to experts and to the adopters. The feedback from this becomes a helpful learning opportunity for the adopters and an assessment tool for social workers. With permission it could also be discussed with referees.

Materials

- A video/DVD camera and playback facilities.

Preparing the exercise

Preparing for this exercise firstly involves social workers tackling their own reservations: it is rare that assessors set such difficult hurdles for their adopters to overcome. However, the rationale was discussed in the introduction to this workbook. Steel yourself!

Set the ground rules. Tell the adopters that:

- this will not be an easy exercise;

- they will not necessarily be given all the information;

- the exercise provides an opportunity to learn more about themselves;

- it will not be used to humiliate them;

- they will be filmed so that good use is made of the experience through feedback;

- with their permission, the film may be discussed with their referee/s;

- there are no right or wrong answers or ways of doing things.

Alternative exercises

1   Set an individual task with the partner present. Ask one partner to do something:

   a)   of which they are afraid, e.g. touch a frog, spider or worm, or walk across a high bridge;

   b)   or which they dislike – e.g. eat a particular food;

   c)   or which they don't feel confident about doing, e.g. bake fairy cakes, with a group of six-year-olds;

   d)   or which they don't often do, e.g. cook their partner a meal.

   All of these can be stressful to individuals. Observe how the partner gives support. Ask how it would have felt without the partner there to help.

2   Set timed joint tasks:

   a)   A *competitive* task, e.g. a game of Scrabble or a round of Mini-golf;

   b)   A *co-operative* activity, e.g. map-reading around an unfamiliar part of town.

3   Other stressful activities involving children might include putting the adopters in charge of a bouncy castle, a tea party, an arts and crafts session or a treasure hunt. Managing several children would be particularly important for people with existing children or people interested in adopting siblings.

4   Show the filmed stress-activity to a referee and ask them to comment on the couple's response – is this typical? How does the applicant normally tackle stressful situations? Who tries to placate whom? Who takes the lead?

5   Set up the communication exercise using a colleague or friend – maybe someone of a different language background or with a communication difficulty. Ask the adopter to find out five key pieces of information, e.g. Are you married? Do you have children? Which is your family's place of origin? What job do you do? What do you enjoy doing in your leisure time?

6   If all else fails, ask a colleague to use role-play.

7   Ask the adopters to play charades: this demonstrates creativity in communicating under pressure when words are disallowed.

8   Try this communication exercise. Using partners, privately give one person a simple message and ask the partner to discover what this information is. The person with the message is allowed to respond to the questioning only with head movements (nods and shakes) – not with words or pointing. You will find that both partners experience frustration and that it takes a long time to get anywhere. Giving a time limit – say, ten minutes – heightens the pressure.

The message might be: 'You were in a shop and your wheelchair accidentally knocked over a pile of tins – now you feel very upset'; or 'You have had an itchy spot on your back for several days and you can't scratch it properly. You need someone to do this for you.'

This exercise particularly emphasises the skill of asking a logical sequence of simple, closed questions.

Summary of learning points

→ Colleagues may need to be initiated into the purpose of the stress exercise as it is a relatively new technique and may be outside their normal experience.

→ It will be useful to find a stressful exercise that will expose aspects of the couple's relationship, and to take this to another level of stress if necessary.

→ A similar exercise for single applicants without an available supporter would be illuminating; and repeated *with* a friend would inform a useful discussion about using support when under pressure.

→ Setting clear ground rules for this exercise would reduce resistance and contribute to its success.

→ A communication exercise is valuable in exposing both skills and qualities.

→ The experience of uncertainty and vulnerability is useful as a basis for discussion during the home study.

→ Social workers should observe this exercise where possible and use video/DVD footage for feedback to the adopters.

Notes on the assessment task: under pressure exercise

It is suggested that when working with applicants, assessors should use the exercise (or a variant) outlined in each chapter and then, using a photocopied version of this worksheet (which is chapter-specific), reflect on the issues raised by the exercise for the assessment of this particular applicant / couple, and the evidence of suitability it may provide.

1. **How can these "stress" exercises be used to open up certain issues for further exploration? Opportunities might arise to explore:**

    ➜ The impact of feeling personally vulnerable and exposed.

    _____

    _____

    ➜ Self-awareness of behaviour under stress and strategies for managing any problematic reactions.

    _____

    _____

    ➜ The impact of having to respond to a partner's reactions in a stressful situation.

    _____

    _____

    ➜ A range of communication methods for use with adults and children.

    _____

    _____

    ➜ The nature of "difference" and how confident the applicants are about helping to bridge the gap.

    _____

    _____

2. **What evidence might emerge from these exercises about some of the skills and qualities necessary to become an adopter or foster carer, which can be used in the assessment report?**

    The tasks shown here might provide direct evidence about:

    ➜ How the applicant behaves under stress; how resilient they are.

    _____

    _____

➡ The nature of the adults' relationship.

_____

_____

➡ Family dynamics and parenting roles (where the exercise involves existing children).

_____

_____

➡ Their ability to keep calm and think clearly under pressure – to maintain effective functioning and positive relationships.

_____

_____

➡ Whether and how the applicant seeks or uses support.

_____

_____

➡ The applicant's tolerance / patience level.

_____

_____

➡ Their flexibility and creativity.

_____

_____

➡ The applicant's ability to communicate creatively and effectively.

_____

_____

➡ Their ability to convey warmth, reassurance and respect.

_____

_____

➡ The applicant's capacity to be empathetic.

_____

_____

3. **Assessor's self-check: does this exercise provide any specific evidence I need in order to come to a recommendation about this applicant?**

_____

_____

Prompts for in-house discussion: under pressure exercise

This worksheet (which is chapter-specific) can be photocopied and used in a team meeting or other agency forum to stimulate discussion about the exercise and how it may be applied.

- How would you and your colleagues feel about introducing exercises like these? Would it be difficult to persuade colleagues about their value?

  _____

  _____

- What would be the logistical difficulties in setting up tasks like these – including health and safety considerations – and how can they be overcome?

  _____

  _____

- Which feasible alternatives would fulfil the same aims?

  _____

  _____

- Are there any cultural considerations to be taken into account?

  _____

  _____

Chapter 5
Trial parenting exercise

Introduction

Adopters often dismiss the idea of taking children who have certain difficulties without really knowing what it would be like to parent them. This is what prevents so many children from ever having families – the adopters' fear of the unknown and the influence of pre-conceived ideas.

As with any new parent, despite endless reading material and discussions, adopters with no prior experience of child care often have very little idea what it will really be like. Of all the exercises, this is arguably the most ground-breaking – the one which gives adopters their most powerful learning experience, takes social workers outside their normal comfort zone, and provides the most useful assessment material.

Aim of the exercise

The aim of the exercise is to give adopters a hands-on experience of looking after children with special needs, or children for whom it is hard to find a family, in the hope that it will change their perception and challenge some of the stereotypes. It can also be used to explore the idea of the placement of any child outside the adopters' initial range of consideration, for example, a different number of children, or gender. For people who have not parented before, this is a reality check.

The film

What you will see

The resources available to the TV company are beyond those of agencies. However, valuable ideas about extending traditional assessment methodology are floated.

The adopters John and Anthony "borrow" seven-year-old Lily for the weekend. Lily has a heart condition, epilepsy and learning difficulties and still needs nappies. Suma and Albert and their birth children have Kiya to stay for the weekend. Kiya is a young girl who has autism.

The adopters' houses are fitted with CCTV cameras and the footage is observed round the clock from a nearby house. The mothers of the borrowed children and the adopters' social workers monitor the weekend and can intervene if necessary.

You will hear from Rebecca, who is John and Anthony's social worker, from Lily's mother, from Kiya's mother and from Stephen the psychologist.

 Now watch the film

Learning points

1   This exercise provides an unparalleled learning opportunity for adopters – both for those who have never parented, and for people who have concerns about parenting particular "kinds" of children, or about the number of children they could

manage. Rebecca, the social worker, says:

This is a unique experience for us because our assessment is usually based in their home and not actually with a child – so it's very useful for us.

The exercise brings the reality home to people in a very concrete way. Stephen, the psychologist, says:

The whole prospect of parenting is difficult to think about in the abstract...How are you going to know what it will be like unless you have spent some time with children?

It can also unexpectedly raise difficult issues for the adopters, which can then be discussed.

2   This exercise or one of its variants is so important that it should be flagged during the early stages of the applicants' relationship with the agency – probably during preparation groups – so that they can think about how they will arrange to care for children, and to be observed doing so. Ideally this would be in their own home, but it might be in a community setting.

3   The key to getting the most value out of this is to provide the experience *in the adopters' own home*. This is their space with all its resonances of privacy, refuge and relaxation. They need to feel what it's like to have that space – and their time – invaded by a child. It also highlights the things that are going to need to change – in the house, the relationship, and in other domestic and social arrangements.

4   As many of the children who wait a long time for a family are disabled or have special needs, caring for such a child provides an invaluable opportunity for adopters to really think about their capacity to do this. It also offers the chance to learn about the extra vulnerability of disabled children to various forms of abuse (NSPCC, 2003). Both the couples in this chapter had been tentatively considering taking a disabled child, so arrangements are made for John and Anthony to look after Lily, who has a range

of physical and learning disabilities; and for Suma and Albert to take Kiya, who has autism.

It is unlikely that what the adopters learn through this experience could be learned quite so forcefully through more traditional means. They learn that caring for a disabled child can require a lot of patience; some special skills; and, most importantly, will reduce the time available for other aspects of their life – including other children. They also experience pleasure when their affection is reciprocated.

5   There is a major risk, however, that struggling to manage one particular disabled child will mean that they say "no" to all others. The social worker will need to stress that each child is an individual, and unlike any other.

6   For inexperienced parents, people can learn through this exercise that children turn your life upside down, and again that looking after any child takes a great deal of time – often far more than anticipated. John, who keeps horses, says:

Lily has got to come before the animals. At the moment our lifestyle does not fit around a child at all, but I know exactly what I'm going to do to make it work – the child will come first; dogs, horses, Anthony – me last.

7   Equally important is that, according to their social worker Rebecca, the experience gives John and Anthony confidence about their potential abilities as parents – confidence that they would not have gained simply through discussion.

8   It is also particularly valuable for the social worker to actually see childless applicants with children. Rebecca, for example, saw evidence of John's nurturing, caring side which she had not witnessed before.

9   It is difficult for childless couples to appreciate what it *feels* like to be responsible for a child – to know that "the buck stops here". In the film you can see John really taking on board the huge

responsibility of getting Lily's medication right. There is also the unexpected way that a child can trigger feelings of fondness and attachment. None of this can be conveyed with sufficient impact except by actually doing the caring. John reflects on how caring for Lily gave him an inkling of how it would feel to be a father '...*and it was a nice feeling*'. At the end of the weekend, John says:

This has taught me and Anthony so much – it really has. It's a shame that all those future adoptive parents out there don't get a chance to do what we've done, because they are going into it cold.

10 A subsidiary point is that there is a huge difference between managing children in a professional capacity (as Anthony does as a teacher) and what it feels like to be *in loco parentis* in your own home – how you think and behave, how the dynamics of existing relationships alter, how you react when you are tired, and so on. Quite a few prospective adopters work with children in schools or the health service, and this difference must be acknowledged and explored. It is risky to take the short cut and extrapolate from the professional domain to the personal: new evidence is needed about the adopter's personality and capacities with children in their domestic setting.

11 The partner relationship can undergo re-evaluation because each person is seeing the other in a new role and therefore in a new light. This may have positive results or negative, but is an invaluable learning opportunity for the applicants: better to know and explore these things in advance rather than after a new child is placed. In John and Anthony's case, what is discovered about John is positive. Anthony says that watching John has been: '...*a revelation – he's really enjoying himself – you can see he loves doing things for people.*' A useful follow-up would be to pose the same question to John, about Anthony.

12 It can also be illuminating for the assessing social worker to see how a couple copes with this new and demanding situation together. It is a real-life stress test. For Rebecca, what she witnessed with John and Anthony was reassuring and provided evidence which she could use in her assessment report.

13 For couples who already have a family, it provides a chance for adopters to reflect on the impact another child might have on their children. Research shows that placing a child with an established family is a considerable risk factor in adoption (Quinton *et al*, 1998), so the reality must be tested before a placement is made. The needs of Kiya, who spends the weekend with Suma and Albert's family, would have provided the couple and their social worker with much food for thought. Although only a small snapshot, we witness how the birth children attempt to engage but then are silent and watchful as their mother copes with Kiya's demands.

The body language of the family during the debriefing at the end of the weekend (particularly their son, and Suma, who is half-turned away from David the interviewer) suggests that through this experience they might now be wary about taking a child with Kiya's level of needs. They would then need to consider whether any child would pose a threat to their existing dynamics, or only a child who made exceptional demands as a disabled child might, or a child with particular difficulties.

14 It is often wondered how domestic pets will react when a child comes into the home. This is a good opportunity to observe the reality of this, and to discuss safeguards.

15 Debriefing the adopter immediately afterwards and a couple of weeks later will provide useful material for further discussion. Debrief a couple separately and then compare accounts.

Into practice

Method

This is readily acknowledged to be the most challenging exercise for agencies to replicate. The necessary safeguards and observation methods required for a stranger-child to be placed with prospective adopters are beyond the resources of agencies – and are only possible in the extraordinary circumstances of a media-funded documentary. However, there are alternatives.

As the principal aim of this television series and training film is to broaden adopters' view about the kinds of children they could take, and to feel more confident about this, it is important that a borrowed child reflects aspects of the kind of child / children whom the adopters might automatically reject as a match. At the start of the process, John and Anthony had ruled out the idea of a disabled child so they gained two experiences through this exercise: childcare in general and caring for Lily, a disabled child, in particular. It could be, of course, that adopters need to experience a sibling group.

Preparing the exercise

- Clearly, any children who are borrowed need careful explanations and preparation, with a period of gradual introductions beforehand.

- If this hands-on experience is provided through visits to schools and playgroups, these must only happen after expectations are clarified and all parties are happy about the arrangement.

- For any variation, make sure everyone understands that:

  - the adopters are fully aware of safeguarding issues and safe caring (see the 14 "issues to consider" in Chapman, 2009, p 50);

  - the at-home visits are normally arranged between friends and are not the responsibility of the local authority;

  - household health and safety advice is available (see Chapman, 2009, pp 47–49 for a sample checklist);

  - everyone is clear about boundaries and rules.

Alternative exercises

1   Right at the start of the preparation process, introduce the need for the applicants to demonstrate hands-on care of children. This provides unparalleled insights for them and a wealth of evidence for the assessor. If the idea is introduced early enough, there will be plenty of time for this to be arranged. Some agencies now tell their applicants that they will not be taken to panel and/or that they are unlikely to have children placed with them unless they do this. Prompts and support around arranging this can be given at regular intervals during the preparation process.

The experience can take place either in a community setting or in the applicant's own home, or both. Evidence about how the adopters conduct themselves can be collected from the group leaders and from the assessor's direct observations.

a)   With the usual safeguards, *childless* applicants could:

  - arrange to do some regular voluntary work in a community setting, such as Brownies, Scouts, a football club, special school, a nursery or playgroup, youth group or family centre;

  - identify a relative's or friend's child, and arrange for a gradual progression of care to be organised, rather like the introductions when a "to be adopted" child is identified. They should start with taking limited but increasing levels of responsibility in the child's own home to finally having the child to stay with them for the weekend. Detailed feedback from the child's parent/s will be required plus direct fly-on-the-wall observation by the assessing social worker.

If the applicants envisage taking siblings, the exercise must include more than one child.

b) Applicants with *existing children* can be observed at home, but arranging for an extra child to stay the weekend would also be necessary. The family's own children must, of course, be carefully prepared. If the applicants are interested in adopting siblings, ask them to arrange to look after two or three extra children at the same time in their home.

In any scenario where someone is observing the situation, make sure that the children know that it is not they who are under scrutiny.

2 For adopters with older existing children, ask them to invite a school friend for the weekend and set the family some tasks, e.g. a shopping expedition. Or time the exercise to coincide with an exchange visit by a foreign student. Debrief the children and the adopters separately afterwards.

3 CCTV coverage is not possible, but during any of the above scenarios, set a task which you will arrange to observe as a fly-on-the-wall. This could be a baking session or an hour or so of family board-games, or just a family mealtime.

4 If relationships are made with community groups (as in 1a above) the agency could consider building on this to forge stronger and more regular links. This is explored again in the following chapter. An incidental advantage might be that the adults running these facilities may at some point become interested in adoption or fostering – or at least in spreading the word.

Summary of learning points

→ This exercise provides both an unparalleled learning opportunity for adopters as well as a unique assessment tool – preparation and assessment together.

→ Experiencing a child is all the more powerful when this happens on home territory.

→ Having to consider the needs of one disabled child provides a great deal of personal learning and invaluable subject matter for a home study discussion.

→ Social workers must ensure that this experience is not taken to be a predictor for looking after any other disabled child, or child who has particular difficulties.

→ For adopters who have never cared for a child this exercise provides a massive learning curve – but, if successfully completed, can significantly increase confidence.

→ It provides the opportunity for adopters to experience caring for two or even three children and to learn from this.

→ It conveys not just the logistical complexities of the task but what it feels like to be a parent.

→ The differences between being professionally involved with children and being a parent can be explored.

→ Observing the exercise provides social workers with invaluable assessment material.

→ This is a unique chance for partners to re-evaluate how the dynamics of their relationship (or the family's relationships) might be affected by the introduction of a new child, and to gain new insights into each other.

→ It provides a window into the potential impact on the family's existing children – which will be a key factor in the success or otherwise of a placement.

→ If the household has pets, this is an opportunity to observe how the animals cope with a child around, and to discuss safety issues.

→ Debrief the experience carefully and use the information as a basis for further discussion.

Notes on the assessment task: trial parenting exercise

It is suggested that when working with applicants, assessors should use the exercise (or a variant) outlined in each chapter and then, using a photocopied version of this worksheet (which is chapter-specific), reflect on the issues raised by the exercise for the assessment of this particular applicant / couple, and the evidence of suitability it may provide.

1. **How can this exercise be used to open up certain issues for further exploration?**

   It may offer opportunities to explore:

   → The risk of generalising from this intensive experience with one particular child. Although some issues remain generic, other children will present distinct and different challenges.

   _____

   _____

   → The effects on the applicant's existing lifestyle, activities, relationships and domestic environment.

   _____

   _____

   → What it feels like to be responsible for a child; the measures needed to protect a child from harm.

   _____

   _____

   → Factors which make disabled children more vulnerable to abuse and discrimination, and how to protect them.

   _____

   _____

   → What general risks exist in the domestic and immediate environment and how they can be minimised.

   _____

   _____

   → How the pressures on the adult's relationship/s can be reduced and what supports might be necessary to help with this.

   _____

   _____

   → The facilities and resources that are available in the area. This is easier to think about once the needs of a real child have become apparent during this exercise.

   _____

   _____

→ The particular cultural background of children and how resources will need to be identified to meet those specific needs.

_____

_____

→ How to handle unwanted questions or comments from members of the public.

_____

_____

→ How confidentiality can be maintained whilst the child has an acceptable "cover story".

_____

_____

_____

2. **What evidence might emerge from this exercise about some of the skills and qualities necessary to become an adopter or foster carer, which can be used in the assessment report?**

The trial parenting exercise may provide direct evidence about:

→ The applicant's ability to cope with stress and conflicting demands.

_____

_____

→ Their ability to work closely with others in the child's best interests.

_____

_____

→ How the applicant copes with the day-to-day logistics of caring for a child or children.

_____

_____

→ Their ability to relate to and nurture a particular child to a good standard.

_____

_____

→ The applicant's ability both to set boundaries and to be appropriately permissive whilst conveying acceptance and affection.

_____

_____

→ Their ability to listen and to communicate clearly according to the child's age and understanding.

_____

_____

→ The extent to which the applicants work as a team, using time and skills flexibly.

_____

_____

→ Their ability to maintain caring relationships with their partner or existing family members whilst attending to the child's needs.

_____

_____

→ Conversely, how good they are at prioritising the child's needs when faced with competing demands.

_____

_____

→ The observed impact on existing children and how the applicants manage this.

_____

_____

→ The extent to which the current domestic and wider environment is suitable for children.

_____

_____

3. **Assessor's self-check: does this exercise provide any specific evidence I need in order to come to a recommendation about this applicant?**

   It is evident that this particular exercise offers many triggers for further discussion during the home study, and a wide range of evidence to use in the assessment report.

   _____

   _____

   _____

   _____

Prompts for in-house discussion: trial parenting exercise

This worksheet (which is chapter-specific) can be photocopied and used in a team meeting or other agency forum to stimulate discussion about the exercise and how it may be applied.

- What would assessors learn using the method shown in the film which they could not learn in other ways?

_____

_____

- What would be the logistical difficulties in setting up a task like this and how might they be overcome?

_____

_____

- Which feasible alternative would fulfil the same aims?

_____

_____

- Would protocols for the visit be useful? For example, an outline of the purpose, expectations and conduct of the visit and a structured feedback sheet? Who will devise these?

_____

_____

- In what other ways can this reality be brought home to applicants' other children?

_____

_____

- Are there any cultural considerations to be taken into account?

_____

_____

Chapter 6
Tailor-made experiences

Introduction

This workbook has been following the progress of prospective adopters through preparation and assessment and now the time has come when they are nearer to being matched with children. However, some of the adopters are nervous about the descriptions they are coming across in the children's profiles.

Aim of the exercise

This exercise will be a tailor-made experience. The aim is to "demystify the scary words" by using visits to special schools or youth groups to demonstrate more fully the implications of certain conditions mentioned in the profile of a child under consideration. Hopefully, this will reassure adopters about the potential match.

Because of the risk factor where there are already birth children or adoptive children in the family, this tailor-made experience must include them.

The film

What you will see

In this chapter of the film you will see adopters visiting a dance group and a special school – and really getting involved.

- Cathy and Richard visit *So Dancers* – a mixed group of not-disabled children and children with additional needs, including both physical disabilities and learning

difficulties. They take with them their daughter Rachel. The couple at this point are being considered for a child who is being tested for various syndromes. They have a chat with Victoria, a 17-year-old young woman with Down's syndrome, so they can get a sense of how independent disabled people can be.

- Rachel, the adopter, is being considered for a boy who has some behavioural difficulties and she is worried about how she might cope. She visits a school for children with challenging behaviour and is asked to take a hands-on role with the class.

You will hear from the adopters, from Stephen the psychologist and from Teresa, Rachel's social worker.

 Now watch the film

Learning points

1 Cultivating links with a variety of special schools or community groups would pave the way for observation visits of this kind to become a standard part of preparation and assessment. As mentioned in the previous chapter, an incidental advantage of forging such links might be that the organisations become advocates for adoption and fostering – even valuable recruiting grounds.

2 An exercise like this helps adopters to see past the stereotype. Cathy and Richard say that they are reassured by what they have learned during their visit, particularly through talking to Victoria whom they are surprised to discover is involved in quite

"normal" activities. They also learn that '*in some cases these children can eventually look after themselves to a degree*'. Richard says the whole experience was '*Quite an eye-opener*'.

Rachel, the adopter who visits the special school, says:

When you think about children with "behavioural problems" you have all these visions of kids tearing around and swearing – and actually it was quite straightforward in the end.

3   Visits like these would provide what Richard described as 'an eye-opener' for all applicants and ideally should be a standard part of every preparation programme, regardless of whether or not people say they are interested in disability.

4   Birth children and already-adopted children in the family are certain to gain from this exercise too. On the visit to the dance group, Rachel (Cathy and Richard's daughter) overcomes her reluctance and joins in the activities. This is a learning opportunity for her as well.

5   Putting adopters into situations where they can experience a wide spectrum of abilities and disabilities has the potential to expand their views about accepting a child who may be on the less extreme end of the spectrum – but nevertheless a child whom previously they would not have considered at all.

6   Adopters can gain confidence from negotiating unfamiliar environments. They may be surprised to discover that they do have the personal capacities to meet such challenges. For example, look how relaxed Rachel (the adopter) has become with the group of children in the special school.

Teresa, the social worker, says that watching professionals in these environments can also give adopters reassurance, confidence and useful tips about management.

7   Teachers and other staff are in a good position to provide feedback to social workers about the visit as long as this has all been negotiated beforehand. It may be that direct observation by the assessing social worker is too intrusive, but this could be explored.

8   Even better would be for the social worker to be an impassive, fly-on-the-wall observer and concentrate on some of the more subtle indications of the impact of this experience. For example, it is evident from Cathy's and Richard's responses that, although they willingly participate in the activities, and seem to be having fun, they are still cautious and their doubts may need further exploration. Rachel's visit to the special school, on the other hand, appears to have had a very positive impact.

9   As with the trial parenting, a full debrief of this exercise is very important. In Chapter 5 it was suggested that debriefing should happen immediately afterwards and then a couple of weeks later; and that debriefing a couple separately and then comparing accounts could be illuminating.

Into practice

Method

When a potential match is mooted, find out what, if anything, is causing the prospective adopters to be concerned. Pinpoint an institution (or devise an experience) that will throw light on the particular issue in a realistic way, and arrange a visit (accompanied or unaccompanied). Afterwards, debrief all parties as necessary.

Preparing the exercise

Visits arranged for the benefit of prospective adopters will need to take into account the following:

- That all police disclosure checks on the visiting adults are in place and up to date (remember that an adopter may wish to take a friend or relative as a supporter).

- That confidentiality is ensured for children and for the adopter, with the usual *caveats* and safeguards.

- That the institution and the adopter have a clear understanding of the purpose of the visit and how it will be conducted, e.g. as observer or participant.

- That timing is agreed so that key timetable events are included or avoided as necessary.

- That a transparent feedback mechanism is agreed so that the visit can be subsequently discussed in a purposeful way between the social worker and the adopter (a pro-forma may be helpful).

Alternative exercises

1   As many children awaiting adoption have special needs of one kind or another, particularly those children for whom it is hard to find families, it is a good idea to establish a relationship with:

- a local special school

- an exclusion unit

- a child development centre

- a mainstream school

- a nightclub catering for disabled adolescents.

    An ongoing link would be of potential value not just to social workers, but also to staff in these institutions, who could be invited to training sessions and briefings to learn more about looked after and adopted children.

2   Invite Heads and SENCOs (Special Education Needs Co-ordinators) from local special schools to speak at a session of the adopters' preparation groups. Make this a regular part of the preparation, not just an optional add-on for those interested in disabled children. This will reinforce links and make arranging visits much easier.

3   Look out for other local facilities and institutions in the community, such as art groups, youth clubs, activity groups for disabled young people, churches, Sunday schools and faith groups.

4   Consider routinely including a paediatrician in the preparation groups to talk about:

- developmental delay

- the effects of maternal drugs / alcohol

- the physiological effects of neglect

5   Make a point of accompanying the adopters on a visit and observe how they conduct themselves under pressure: what values it reveals; how they relate to the children; how respectful they are to the staff – and so on.

Summary of learning points

→   Try to cultivate links with special schools and youth groups.

→   This exercise is a good way for adopters to see past the stereotypes which blight the placement chances of so many children.

→   It may expand the range of children whom the adopters feel comfortable about considering.

→   It can provide an excellent learning opportunity for existing children in the family.

→   Working alongside professionals in an unfamiliar environment can give confidence and provide good models of how to manage particular situations.

→   Feedback and debriefing will provide the social worker with further issues for exploration with the family.

Notes on the assessment task: tailor-made experiences

It is suggested that when working with applicants, assessors should use the exercise (or a variant) outlined in each chapter and then, using a photocopied version of this worksheet (which is chapter-specific), reflect on the issues raised by the exercise for the assessment of this particular applicant / couple, and the evidence of suitability it may provide.

1. How can this exercise be used to open up certain issues for further exploration?

It may offer opportunities to explore:

→ The applicant's understanding of certain terms and diagnoses; the range of ability / disability within the term and some of the lifestyle consequences for the child and for the prospective adopters / foster carers.

_____

_____

→ The level of understanding of other children in the family.

_____

_____

→ Their feelings about living alongside disability or difference.

_____

_____

→ The appropriateness of the family's accommodation and any neighbourhood issues.

_____

_____

→ The financial impact of taking on the care of a disabled child.

_____

_____

→ The applicant's acceptance of the likely need for support and their willingness to seek it; the role of people identified on their eco-map.

_____

_____

→ The availability of community facilities and resources appropriate to the particular child in mind, with particular reference to the Assessment Framework (if in England or Wales).

_____

2. **What evidence might emerge from this exercise about some of the skills and qualities necessary to become an adopter or foster carer, which can be used in the assessment report?**

   This exercise may provide direct evidence about:

   → The applicant's attitude to diversity and willingness to accept children and young people for what they are.

   _____

   _____

   → Their commitment to the process and their reliability in complying with arrangements and working with others.

   _____

   _____

   → Their sensitivity as guests in a new environment with unfamiliar people.

   _____

   _____

   → Their flexibility of approach and willingness to explore new things and take personal risks for the greater good.

   _____

   _____

   → Their capacity to listen, co-operate, relate to others and communicate with children and young people.

   _____

   _____

   → The applicant's ability to set boundaries and manage children's behaviour appropriately.

   _____

   _____

3. **Assessor's self-check: does this exercise provide any specific evidence I need in order to come to a recommendation about this applicant?**

   _____

   _____

Prompts for in-house discussion: tailor-made experiences

This worksheet (which is chapter-specific) can be photocopied and used in a team meeting or other agency forum to stimulate discussion about the exercise and how it may be applied.

• What can you do to establish or strengthen links with schools and community groups?

_____

_____

• Would protocols for visits be useful? For example, an outline of the purpose, expectations and conduct of the visit (all parties) and a structured feedback sheet? Who will devise these?

_____

_____

• What are the risks / drawbacks and how might these be overcome?

_____

_____

• Are there any cultural considerations to be taken into account?

_____

_____

Conclusion

In *Adopted Children Speaking* there is the following passage:

> One girl said she had had to wait five years [for a family]. When she was asked what the waiting was like she answered:
> Terrible! I wait, I wait, I wait, I wait...
> I wait for the telephone to ring every day...
> No news...until my fifth year.
> (Thomas and Beckford, 1991, p 40)

The very idea of children "waiting, waiting, waiting" for permanent new families should keep us all awake at night. The fact that the number is still so high should be the spur to tackle this desperate situation through whatever means can be devised, however unfamiliar and demanding.

Basically a much wider pool of adopters and permanent foster carers is needed who can understand the range of children waiting for families, and can demonstrate that they are robust enough to take up the challenges. So family placement workers have a two-fold task: to open up the imaginations of those who come forward in order that they will consider taking children they had never dreamed about; and to assess them rigorously against the requirements of the job ahead. As discussed in the introduction, for prospective families this is a developmental journey on no modest scale.

But the journey must be taken by staff as well as families. Although the hill to be climbed by the adopters and foster carers is steep, it is the social workers who may find the going particularly tough. Ideas may be accepted in principle, but staffing is short, resources are scarce and energy is frequently diverted elsewhere. But the rewards for embracing this challenge are immense. The agencies that were engaged in the TV series which gave rise to this training film attest to the way their practice in preparation and assessment has been reinvigorated. Challenges, it seems, can also be stimulants.

The techniques shown in this film, if implemented, will almost certainly impact on practice even if this is via their many variants described in this workbook. Each chapter will provide almost endless material for team discussion and, it is hoped, revitalised experimentation. Perhaps the most powerful message comes from the "trial parenting" chapter, which mainly follows the progress of John and Anthony's experience with Lily. As with all the exercises, this is raw, taxing, hands-on experience, not hypothetical discussion. Having watched the film, it will seem self-evident that this kind of exercise is central to the task of assessing both childless people and people who already have children.

When it comes to matching, a demonstrably robust preparation and assessment process, with all the evidence it generates, will almost inevitably enhance the families' chances of being matched. The greater the challenge, the higher can be the expectations. More children with extra needs will therefore get placements. Placing agencies can be confident that the families are properly prepared, and, incidentally, that an agency which demonstrates such good practice is likely to take its support role very seriously.

There is no question that the key to the success of these innovations will be the confidence and enthusiasm conveyed by the agency. All parties need to know that there is a rationale for putting staff and prospective families into situations where at times they may feel uncomfortable; but that the methods do work and the effort is worth it. With a strong message like this, families' confidence will also be boosted.

Where everyone together is pushing the boundaries, children will ultimately reap the benefits.

Chapter 8
Case studies

These are sample case studies which can be used for the exercises in Chapter 2. They are based on the real experiences and backgrounds of children, though names and identifying details have been changed.

Case studies are different from profiles.

Profiles are used to feature real children widely for family-finding purposes. They are a very effective way of securing links with adopters and permanent foster carers for many hundreds of children every year. Although the profiling newspaper *Be My Parent* and its online version www.bemyparent.org.uk, and Adoption UK's magazine, *Children Who Wait,* are subscriber publications, their circulation can include a wider public. They are seen by the children themselves, and can come into the hands of people who know them. Once they are published, they can, of course, become part of the child's memory box. For this reason, in profiles, some of the very personal details are usually omitted in order to protect the children's (and their birth family's) privacy and dignity.

Case studies, on the other hand, are used as training material and are public documents. The children described are to some extent fictitious composites of actual children, and highly personal issues can be included for discussion purposes. However, all the situations and experiences described are themselves absolutely real, and have happened – are happening – to children regularly.

The case studies offered here for training purposes are deliberately ethnically neutral. The reason for this was discussed in the introduction.

Case study 1

Jo (2½ years) and Jay (1 year)

Jo enjoys quiet games with his foster carers and is always keen to please them. At first he followed them around anxiously but is now more confident about playing with other children. The ideal treat for Jo is when his foster carers take him to the park with several of the neighbours' children.

Jay enjoys music, playing with toys and being in his baby walker. As a baby he was tense and unresponsive but he is now beginning to respond to affection from his carers and to relax. Recently he has started to laugh and chuckle.

History

Jo and Jay have one sibling, a sister Jess, who is four years old. The boys are to be placed together, and will maintain direct contact with Jess who is to be placed separately.

The children have been in care for eight months. While living with their parents, they had a transient lifestyle, never settling long in one place. Sometimes they stayed with relatives; sometimes they slept in a car.

It came to light that the parents were involved in serious criminal activities and the children were removed from their care. The parents are now in prison.

All three children were emotionally and physically neglected, and there is evidence that Jess was sexually abused. All the children have witnessed violent and frightening incidents.

Jo has displayed inappropriate sexualised behaviour, and it is thought that he is likely to need therapeutic help in the future.

Case study 2

Aaron (7 years)

Aaron is a lively boy, tall for his age and quite sturdy. He loves riding his bike and making dens. Although Aaron enjoys building Lego castles with his foster carer, he tends to have a short attention span and can lose interest quite quickly. He needs to be the centre of attention and can be very demanding.

Aaron has periodic severe asthma (for which he takes medication) and a tendency to get bronchitis, which makes it worse, and tonsillitis. His development lags behind that of his peers in some areas and he has difficulty with speech and language. He has been referred to the hearing clinic.

History

Aaron has been with his foster family for 18 months. Prior to this, while in his mother's care, he lived in many places and was left with a variety of different people, experiencing considerable instability and confusion. There was very little routine, supervision or boundary-setting. His mother was able to meet very few of his emotional, social or developmental needs.

Aaron has started to feel able to trust his foster carers and is beginning to form a tentative attachment to them. However, due to the extreme chaos which characterised his early life, he will need play therapy to help him develop relationships, make sense of his life experiences and understand why he is unable to live with his birth family.

Case study 3

Donna (6 years)

Donna is often found quietly playing with her dolls, and needs encouragement to play with other children. She can be quite slow to do things and needs lots of support, though she can become confused and angry if anyone tries to help her. Donna tends to fret a lot about scrapes and bruises and sometimes scratches herself to create marks.

History

Donna has been in care for a year. It is thought that prior to this she was looked after by nine different people. Donna's mother, Bel, misuses alcohol, and may have been doing so during her pregnancy with Donna. Bel has long-standing mental health difficulties. On several occasions she threatened to kill Donna and then commit suicide.

The family home was cold, dirty and untidy; there were no covers on the beds, which were mattresses on the floor. Donna was badly neglected – unwashed, with dirty, inadequate clothing – and at times she went without food. It was noted that she repeatedly had severe untreated conjunctivitis. In many respects, Donna was expected to care for herself. On one occasion she was found wandering the streets alone late at night. At school she was becoming aggressive to the other children.

After coming into care Donna disclosed that she had been sexually abused by her mother and by her grandmother's partner.

Donna has a habit of biting her lips and picking at her hands, which are sore from being deliberately kept under the tap for a long time. A child psychiatrist who has assessed Donna has advised ongoing therapy.

Donna is settling well with her foster carers. She is beginning to make progress at school and is making friendships. She says she would like a new mummy and daddy and a brother or sister.

Case study 4

Ana (8 years) and Abi (5½ years)

Ana is a sensitive, rather guarded child who does not make friends easily. She seems "old for her age". She lacks confidence and has low self-esteem, which can show itself in difficult behaviour.

Ana struggles to concentrate at school, and copes best with quiet activities like painting. Although she is wary of trying new things, she has just started to learn the recorder.

Abi is an energetic and inquisitive child with a rather overbearing manner. She is sociable with adults but needs to be in charge when she plays with other children. She can be strong-willed and defiant and needs firm boundaries. When angry, Abi has been known to hurt the cat belonging to the foster carer's son.

Ana and Abi's relationship is complex. At home, Ana felt responsible for Abi and at times is still over-anxious about her wellbeing. However, they frequently fight with each other quite viciously, while at other times they withdraw into an impenetrable twosome.

History

While living at home, Ana and Abi witnessed violence between their parents, who were also victims of violent crime. Their father was stabbed and the family home was burgled and ransacked on several occasions. The parents' lifestyle included illegal drug use and alcohol misuse. Their mother became intimate with a man known to be risky to children.

Ana and Abi were taken into care. Their frightening and chaotic early experiences meant that neither child learned to develop a trusting relationship with their parents. This means that it will take a long time for them to trust adults and at first it may feel unrewarding to care for them.

It is planned that the girls will have indirect contact with their mother, and possible face-to-face contact with their father.

Case study 5

Connor (4 years)

Connor is a quiet, rather serious little boy who prefers solitary activities. He is fearless, and will try most things. He enjoys the swings in the park, playing with Thomas the Tank Engine and watching cartoons.

Connor has global developmental delay. He functions at around the three-year-old level and still requires nappies. He has speech and language therapy, which is likely to continue.

Connor also has some features suggestive of an autistic spectrum disorder: he has a tendency to rock if he is excited or frustrated, and has difficulty coping with changes in his routine. He is reluctant to wear new clothes, will only eat a restricted range of food, and is prone to tantrums.

History

Connor is one of six siblings, all of whom will be placed in permanent families. The plan for the two oldest is permanent fostering, and for Connor and his younger siblings, adoption.

All the children have been severely neglected, and one of Connor's brothers was sexually abused. Their home was dirty, and there were no clean clothes or nappies for the children. Neighbours reported that they had seen Connor's father hitting the older children. Connor himself was dirty and sore and had blisters round his lower body due to being soaked in urine for long periods. The children used to beg for food from neighbours and sometime forage in waste-paper bins in the street.

The plan is for Connor to be adopted on his own, and to have regular face-to-face contact with his siblings. Indirect contact with his parents is planned.

Case study 6

Mia (3 months)

Mia is a delightful baby girl who readily engages with her carers.

Mia's facial features suggest that she has a form of foetal alcohol syndrome (FAS). She has difficulty sucking and swallowing and it is possible that she may need a temporary naso-gastric tube for feeding. Although her development is significantly delayed currently, it is thought that she will begin to catch up over the next year or so.

In the future, Mia is likely to have difficulties with her ability to concentrate, and she may have other behavioural difficulties.

History

Mia is the youngest of three children. Her two older brothers, one of whom may also have FAS, have been placed for adoption together. It is hoped that Mia will have contact with her brothers in the future.

Both of Mia's parents misuse alcohol and illegal drugs. Both have made efforts to give them up, but have been unsuccessful. The parental relationship was very unpredictable and the children were exposed to episodes of verbal and, occasionally, physical violence between the adults. Their mother's relationship with her extended family is also volatile and complex, which again put the children at risk.

Indirect contact with both parents is envisaged.

Case study 7

Natalia (9 years), Izzi (6½ years) and Finn (5½ years)

Natalia is a rather sad, serious girl who constantly looks for adult approval. With her class teacher's encouragement she has joined the lunchtime choir. Through this she has made one or two friends and is gaining in confidence.

Natalia has some learning difficulties and will need extra support in a mainstream school. She has a very ambivalent relationship with her mother, feeling loved and then rejected unpredictably. She feels responsible for her younger siblings and worries about their wellbeing.

Izzi is more confident than her sister, and loves dancing and music. In the foster home she is eager to please, though can be sulky and moody at times for no apparent reason. Like Natalia, Izzi also has attachment difficulties and would benefit from life story work to help her make sense of her experiences.

Izzi has a dairy-free diet, and will tell you that she cannot drink milk.

Finn is generally a happy little boy who adores his sisters. Finn at times becomes withdrawn and needs to be encouraged to play with his toys. His carer reports that he does not like the word "No", and will cry pitifully even when gently reprimanded.

History

The children's mother has suffered with severe depression throughout their lives, which made the children wary and anxious not to make things worse. The family was often threatened with eviction, and the home was cold and dirty. The children were the subject of considerable emotional abuse and neglect. Their mother blames Natalia for many of the family's problems and yet it is Natalia who is likely to find it the most difficult of all the children to be permanently separated from home.

The plan is for the three children to be placed together in permanent foster care. They will have periodic direct contact with both their parents.

Case study 8

Kieran (10 years)

Kieran is the oldest of three children who are all being placed separately.

Kieran is a reserved boy whose interests centre around computer games and playing with his pet hamsters. It takes him a while to come out of his shell when he meets new people. He has very low self-esteem and will often give up on tasks if he feels he might not be able to complete them. His younger brother teases him about his difficulties with reading and writing, which only contributes to Kieran's reluctance to try.

Kieran needs a family who can love him for himself, but who can accept it may be a long time before he is able to return their affection.

History

At home, the children were shouted at, hit when they did something wrong, and neglected. Kieran's sister was sexually abused by one of their parents' friends. The sister was their mother's favourite, and Kieran was often blamed for any problems and also over-shadowed by his younger brother.

Once the father had left, their mother's learning difficulties meant that it was hard for her to cope alone with the children, especially the boys. After several unsuccessful episodes of "respite" with relatives, she finally requested that the boys be taken into care. There is very little chance of the mother being able to parent her children adequately; the father cannot be found and the relatives are unwilling to offer more support. Care proceedings have therefore been started.

Kieran has been with his present foster carers for only two months after his previous placement disrupted. Although he prefers to be alone he is gradually joining in with family activities.

Case study 9

Sam (4 years)

Sam is a solemn, watchful little boy with mournful eyes. It is all the more delightful when he suddenly chuckles when being played with. He particularly likes hide and seek, which sends him into fits of giggles.

Sam has a number of significant difficulties. He has a slightly oversized head, which appears uneven. He has a condition called Infantile Myofibromatosis, which forms small benign lumps visible on the body and the head. The lumps, which appear and disappear, are usually under the skin, but in some cases can form on internal organs with more serious consequences. At this stage it is not thought that the condition will shorten Sam's lifespan, but he will need medical involvement throughout.

Sam also has a degree of learning difficulty and his speech is very delayed. Other aspects of his development are mostly within the expected range for his age.

History

Sam's mother, Nina, is a single parent who has for a long time been a service user of the local community mental health team. She will not divulge the identity of Sam's father. Nina was very affectionate with Sam as a baby but began to realise that, even with help, she would be unable to offer him all the special care he would need in the future. She wants him to have an adoptive family but she would like to see him from time to time.

After an initial period of wariness, Sam settled well with his foster carers and is now a much-loved part of the family.

Case study 10

Lela (3 years)

Lela presents as an outgoing, inquisitive little girl with curly thick brown hair and hazel eyes. She appears to be a friendly child, though sometimes she can be overwhelming with her affection. It is thought, however, that she is in fact an unhappy little girl who struggles to believe that she is loved. Lela can be aggressive and deny that she did something if she is corrected.

History

Lela is the youngest of four children and throughout her short life there have been concerns about all their safety. The children have different fathers, and the house was known to be visited by a succession of different men. All the children have experienced erratic parenting and physical abuse. There was evidence that Lela had been hit, and there were strangulation marks on her neck. She was deprived of food.

The authorities became aware of the situation following a referral from the RSPCA. The family's Alsatian dogs were out of control and starving.

The children were made the subject of child protection plans, since when they have been in care several times – often split up in different foster homes.

The children are now on care orders and Lela is also the subject of a Placement Order for adoption. There will be indirect contact with the siblings in foster care and with her parents.

Jo (2½ years) and Jay (1 year)

Aaron (7 years)

Donna (6 years)

Ana (8 years) and Abi (5½ years)

Connor (4 years)

Mia (3 months)

Izzi (6½ years), Natalia (9 years) and Finn (5½ years)

Kieran (10 years)

Sam (4 years)

Lela (3 years)

References

Adoption Register for England and Wales (2007) *Adoption Register for England and Wales Annual Report 2006*, London; BAAF.

Beesley P (2009) *Assessing Second-time Adopters*, Practice Note 54, London: BAAF

Be My Parent statistics at www.bemyparent. org.uk/info-for-agencies/statistics/

Be My Parent (2009) *What is Developmental Delay?* Be My Parent, News and Features, Issue 161, September 2009, London: BAAF

Chapman R (2009) *Undertaking a Fostering Assessment: A guide to collecting and analysing information for Form F (Fostering) England,* London: BAAF

Cousins J (2003) 'Are we missing the match? Rethinking adopter assessment and child profiling', *Adoption & Fostering*, 27:4, pp 7–18

Department of Health (2000) *Framework for the Assessment of Children in Need and their Families,* London: The Stationery Office

Harris P (ed) (2008) *The Colours in Me: Writing and poetry by adopted children and young people,* London: BAAF

Ivaldi G (2000) *Surveying Adoption*, London: BAAF

Laming WH (2003) *The Victoria Climbié Inquiry: Report of an inquiry by Lord Laming*, London: The Stationery Office

Leslie A (2001) *Report of the Part 8 Review for Brighton and Hove ACPC of the Care and Protection of JAS (aged 4) who Died on 24th December 1999*, Brighton: Brighton and Hove ACPC

NSPCC (2003) *"It doesn't happen to disabled children": Child protection and disabled children, Report of the National Working Group on Child Protection and Disability,* London: NSPCC

Quinton D, Rushton A, Dance C and Mayes D (1998) *Joining New Families: A study of adoption and fostering in middle childhood,* Chichester: John Wiley and Sons

Selwyn J, Sturgess W, Quinton D and Baxter C (2006) *Costs and Outcomes of Non-Infant Adoptions,* London: BAAF

Selwyn J and Wijedasa D (2009) 'The placement of looked after ethnic minority children', in Schofield G and Simmonds J (eds) *The Child Placement Handbook,* London: BAAF

Simon J and Dance C (2006) *Disabled Children who are Looked After: Local authority survey 1999* summarised by Jennifer Cousins www.baaf.org.uk/about/projects/openingdoors/ researchsummary.pdf

Thomas C and Beckford V (1999) *Adopted Children Speaking,* London: BAAF